TEILHARD DE CHARDIN
ON MORALITY

D1521370

Teilhard de Chardin on Morality

Living in an Evolving World

Louis M. Savary

Paulist Press
New York / Mahwah, NJ

Cover image by Netkoff/Shutterstock.com
Cover and book design by Lynn Else

Library of Congress Cataloging-in-Publication Data
Names: Savary, Louis M., author.
Title: Teilhard de Chardin on morality : living in an evolving world / Louis M. Savary.
Description: New York : Paulist Press, 2019. | Includes bibliographical references and index.
Identifiers: LCCN 2018042719 (print) | LCCN 2018056113 (ebook) | ISBN 9781587687846 (ebook) | ISBN 9780809154074 (pbk. : alk. paper)
Subjects: LCSH: Teilhard de Chardin, Pierre. | Christian ethics—Catholic authors. | Creationism.
Classification: LCC BX4705.T39 (ebook) | LCC BX4705.T39 S28 2019 (print) | DDC 241/.042092—dc23
LC record available at https://lccn.loc.gov/2018042719

ISBN 978-0-8091-5407-4 (paperback)
ISBN 978-1-58768-784-6 (e-book)

Published by Paulist Press
997 Macarthur Boulevard
Mahwah, New Jersey 07430
www.paulistpress.com

Printed and bound in the
United States of America

Contents

Contents

Preface

MODERN SCIENCE, evolutionary theories, and innovative technology have significantly expanded our intellectual horizons. Scientific findings continue to offer new insights into the mysteries of our universe and ourselves. For people of faith, such new knowledge helps reveal deeper truths about the wonder-filled world that God created for us. This is the evolving world we were given to manage responsibly. The flow of new knowledge also provides a constantly expanding foundation for our spiritual and moral lives.

This book sets out to explain the ethical thinking of French Jesuit Pierre Teilhard de Chardin (1881–1955). Hopefully, it will help people reframe and reshape their conscience in light of evolving contemporary knowledge. We have come to realize that Earth is far more than a waiting room for heaven, as many believers in previous generations were taught.

Today, we are challenged to recognize Earth in many new ways: as a giant workplace where we learn to assemble and create our future; as a laboratory where we can explore and test our new ideas; as a stage on which to perform our roles and live out our life's purpose; as a family home where we grow in love and compassion; as a classroom and school of experience and self-development; as a playground of wonders to delight and inspire us; as a cosmic neighborhood of exotic planets yet to visit; and as a sacred space provided by God to nurture our spirits. Yes, it is all of them at the same time!

Morally, we are called today to think in cosmic dimensions, yet never to forget the little everyday acts of thoughtfulness and caring that form the staple diet of normal human existence. As scientific film director James Marsh stated, "We don't need cosmic alibis to absolve us from our daily responsibilities and moral choices."[1]

Each year, we continue to comprehend more and more how

our universe came to exist and how sentient life has been evolving on Earth over the past billion years or so. Scientific discoveries have overturned many traditional beliefs about our planet, our solar system, our galaxy, our universe, and the emergence of humans. Until very recently, much of our moral lives and many of our ethical decisions had been based on more traditional beliefs about the age, size, and makeup of the cosmos, as well as the origins of humanity. Many of these beliefs are at least 400—some even more than 2,400—years old. Teilhard brings us up to date.

In his writings, Teilhard was the first to integrate what we have learned from modern science and evolutionary theory in ways that resonate with Christian theology. For him, the facts and the theological implications of evolution must influence the ways people live out their moral lives. In these pages, we take Teilhard's lead and look at today's ethical challenges regarding an evolving universe, an evolving planet, and an evolving human species.

I have spent the past forty years of my life presenting the remarkable insights of this Jesuit priest. I have written books, taught classes, given lectures, and led workshops to explain his ideas. One continuous challenge has been to clarify his often-difficult writing in ways people can more easily understand and find useful.

Although I may claim to have a good grasp of the way Teilhard thinks, I do not purport to be an expert in the field of moral theology. Nor did Teilhard. I leave any fine-point disagreements and debates over Teilhard's ideas to more academic, ethical philosophers and moral theologians. I am writing primarily for the lay reader.

In these pages, I simply want to present Teilhard's insights and implications for contemporary moral behavior. I use accessible language with examples so that anyone can grasp his ethical principles and put them into practice.

Teilhard's way to live a moral life in today's world is presented for those who feel the need for a new way of responding to the problems of our age. Teilhard would say that it is not enough for people of faith merely to be intellectually curious about modern science and evolution. They need to live their moral lives *evolutely*, that is, by promoting the further development of our planet in whatever ways they can, individually and in collaboration with others. They need to adopt a forward-looking spirituality and to act morally in ways that will keep humanity maturing in heart and mind.

Preface

Teilhard proposes a nontraditional but Christian approach to morality and ethical issues. He uses modern scientific discoveries and the theory of evolution as well as New Testament writings to offer readers an integrative framework for making contemporary ethical choices, individually and collectively.

This Teilhard book on morality is needed, especially for people of faith. Not having a satisfactory alternative ethical approach, many contemporary believers have continued using a "traditional conscience," provided by the church, which has remained essentially unchanged over the past millennium. That traditional ethical conscience is waiting, not to be jettisoned, but to be reshaped and re-envisioned, because a new consciousness of evolving creation is undeniably emerging in our time.

A new consciousness emerges when new knowledge challenges or transcends the old. A new conscience is needed when new knowledge forces us to rethink what we have traditionally believed to be true not only about our moral life but also about the purposes of God in creation. Teilhard realized that the scientific facts we currently possess about the origins of the universe and evolution of human life force us to shift the very basis of traditional Christian moral theology. Consequently, Teilhard is challenging a morality solidified by the church during the Middle Ages. It was the morality in which he grew up.

For some, Teilhard's evolutionary approach to morality may be difficult to grasp and doubly challenging to put into practice. But there will be many others, hopefully, with whom his moral principles will resonate. Many young people today are trying to develop their own sense of what it means to live a responsible, active moral life in today's world.

As Klaus Schwab, the founder and executive chair of the World Economic Forum observed about the younger generation, "These people have a really global attitude and global identity. To make money is not necessarily their first objective. Their first objective is to make a contribution."[2] Teilhard's ethics of action complement that objective.

Acknowledgments

I AM DEEPLY INDEBTED for insights into Teilhard's morality from three professional Jesuit theologians, Edward Vacek, Robert Faricy, and Roger Haight.

As I was developing my ideas for this book, an article on Teilhard's moral theology, "An Evolving Christian Morality," by Edward Vacek, appeared in a collection of essays in *From Teilhard to Omega* (Orbis, 2014), edited by Ilia Delio. I contacted Fr. Vacek, who agreed to review my work in progress. He provided many helpful and clarifying suggestions and especially reassured me that I was on the right track.

Robert Faricy's comprehensive survey of all aspects of Teilhard's theology, in his *Teilhard de Chardin's Theology of the Christian in the World* (Sheed & Ward, 1967), told me exactly where to look for his ethical material. Faricy's "Index of Topics" saved me perhaps years of sifting through hundreds of Teilhard's essays, panning for small nuggets of his moral insights. Faricy had done most of the prospecting and organized all the gold in his book.

Roger Haight, a fellow classmate in our shared early Jesuit years, has been a mentor and constant guide for almost all the books I've written in this series on Teilhard. No matter how busy he may be, whenever I ask for a favor or help with a new manuscript, he is there. He is the one I count on to catch my more important philosophical or theological inaccuracies.

Susie Timchak, theological graduate student, has read this manuscript in detail, and has made hundreds of small improvements in grammar, alternate word suggestions, matching tenses, rearranging paragraphs, simplifying sentence structure, and catching typos. She has proved to be an invaluable helper.

In the end, I accept responsibility for any errors or misstatements in the text.

For the stories and examples that make my dry prose come alive, I thank my wife, Patricia Berne, who, after reading each section of an early text will inevitably say, "Lou, you need to give the reader an example or a story to make this point clear."

I must also thank my editor, Paul McMahon at Paulist, for his unfailing support and for keeping me challenged. As soon as I send him one manuscript, he gives me suggestions for another new title in this Teilhard series.

I also thank the publishers Harper & Row and Harcourt Brace Jovanovich, who were willing to take a risk in the 1960s and '70s to publish hundreds of Teilhard's essays and talks in English. Their publications provided important material that would otherwise have been unavailable to me and other Teilhard scholars.

As always, I welcome feedback on my books. The problem is that when readers offer great suggestions for improvement, I wish I could modify my manuscript to include their insights. Since revised editions seldom occur these days, I must settle for being deeply grateful that such readers have been moved enough by Teilhard's ideas to write to me.

1

An Emerging Moral Consciousness

TEILHARD NEVER HAD the opportunity to write a book that summarized his ideas on moral theology for contemporary people of faith. He never even wrote an entire essay dedicated to the ethical life. There is no one place where he fully develops his thoughts about sin and its origins, social justice, ecological attitudes, religious life, ethical imperatives, interfaith issues, and many other moral theology topics.[1]

To assemble—or even sketch—any kind of system of his moral thought, one must sift through his various writings. The process involves searching for passages that reflect bits of his thinking about new foundations of morality and suggestions concerning ethical choices and behavior.

Since Teilhard died in 1955, the world has experienced an avalanche of scientific and technological breakthroughs that he perhaps never dreamed of. Some of these are space travel, the World Wide Web, smartphones, robots and drones, mapping of the human genome, gene-splicing, 3D printing, virtual reality, dark energy, and dark matter. Spectacular advances have been made in astronomy, medicine, solar energy production, information storage, nanoscience, paleobiology, and a host of other fields that didn't exist in Teilhard's day. While these advances provide new opportunities for exploration, they also pose new ethical decisions.

Since Teilhard's death, we have also generated many larger moral challenges than any he had to face. These include global warming, rivers and lakes polluted by industrial wastes, worldwide terrorism, multinational corporations, women's equality versus age-old male privilege in political and corporate life, societal integration of the homosexual and transgender populations, violent racial and religious prejudice, the ability to preserve and save human life in premature infants and the elderly but at tremendous financial cost, millions of refugees seeking new homes in nations unwilling or unable to absorb them, sophisticated drug smuggling and human trafficking, antibiotic research unable to keep pace with bacterial mutation, genetic engineering, recombinant DNA technology, biological cryogenics, vast entrenched discrepancies of wealth across the globe, the prevalence of gratuitous violence and sexuality in the media, addictions to computer games or social media, eavesdropping drones, self-replicating robots, computer hacking, and many more.

In many ways, our traditional moral consciousness with its basic ethical rules appears to be inadequate to deal with many of these moral complexities as they continue to emerge. They require a higher level of moral consciousness. Just as in the realm of mathematics, we cannot expect the elementary rules of arithmetic to solve an algebraic equation or to prove a theorem in calculus, so in the realm of the moral life, we cannot expect a static moral consciousness to resolve the ethical problems posed by a complex evolving humanity.

Albert Einstein recognized this need for a higher ethic, when he wrote, "There's been a quantum leap technologically in our age, but unless there's another quantum leap in human relations, unless we learn to live in a new way towards one another, there will be a catastrophe."

For Teilhard, Einstein, and many others, we need to develop a higher, evolving moral consciousness to deal adequately with the ever-changing subtlety of today's ethical issues. We need a clear set of ethical principles for living in an evolving world. I saw this as the task at hand: to assemble and organize Teilhard's thoughts on morality and ethics.

To begin the task, I collected and arranged Teilhard's basic moral insights and theological principles into a systematic framework. The book then presents some conclusions in the form of ethical principles that express how and what Teilhard might suggest as a set of moral guidelines for the evolving world in which we live.

Through this process, we convey what Teilhard would think or say *as if he were living today*. Thus, despite the book's title, it was not written by Teilhard himself but in the "spirit of Teilhard."

Apparent Contradictions

Henry Cardinal Newman asserted that there can be no contradiction between faith and reason. Faith brings knowledge of God and God's purposes for creation. Reason brings knowledge of creation through the discoveries of science in all its branches. If there arises what seems like an apparent contradiction between what faith says and what science discovers, we cannot say that faith trumps science or that science trumps faith. According to Cardinal Newman, it cannot be an either/or situation, though some would like to see it that way. Such extremists would dismiss either the discoveries of science or discount the tenets of religion. For Cardinal Newman, both forms of knowledge must be integrated. Teilhard heartily agreed.

We must also keep in mind that the New Testament writers relied primarily on the Hebrew Scriptures. As Jews, they were raised religiously to observe the laws enshrined in the first five books of their Bible, called the Torah. In the Torah, Jews found their moral principles and rules for ethical behavior and the foundational tenets of their moral code.

However, there were many additional forms of ritual behavior required by the Torah. These included male circumcision, avoidance of pork, never eating the blood of animals or taking part in the rites of other religions, no sitting down for meals with non-Jews, no work on the Sabbath, and many other dietary and behavioral regulations.

Some of the fiercest moral debates among the first Christian leaders, after Jesus's departure, involved these additional ethical rules. Did one first have to become a Jew to become a Christian? Did a Gentile Christian have to observe all the behavioral rules and regulations of the Torah? Did every Greek male who converted to Christianity have to be circumcised? Could a pagan convert continue to eat meals with his family, if the others were not Christians? Did new Christian converts have to observe all the Jewish food regulations, such as not eating pork? And, more importantly, did a Jew who believed in Jesus as the Messiah have to continue observing all the hundreds of additional regulations listed in the Torah, beyond those that called for love of God and love of neighbor? These debates and conflicts among the early Christians were not about theology. They were primarily about moral behavior.

Debates among the founders of the Christian way of life are important to reflect upon as they gave rise to a newly emerging moral consciousness. They were laying the groundwork for the formation of a new Christian conscience. Teilhard would call the results of these debates an evolutionary advance in moral thinking. He is calling for another evolutionary advance in our day. It may be instructive to reflect upon each side's position in that early Christian dispute, for it may offer us a way to begin to understand today's debate about the newly emerging moral consciousness that Teilhard is proposing.

The First Debate

The founding group of early Christians was centered in Jerusalem and Antioch. Jerusalem was their headquarters. The members of this original believing community were all Jewish. Among them were some of the original apostles, disciples, and close relatives of Jesus. This founding group wanted to require Gentile Christian converts to observe all the requirements of the Torah—in other words, to become converts to Judaism before joining the Christian community.

Paul, an early missionary to the pagan Greeks, took an opposing position. While he was himself a fervent and observant Jew, his moral position about Gentile converts to Christianity differed from those in Jerusalem and Antioch. He held that his Greek converts need *not* undergo circumcision, *nor* did they need to observe all the other minute regulations of the Torah. Paul's argument was that faith in Jesus Christ as Messiah and following his way was all that was required in a convert. In Paul's mind, to insist that observing the Torah was equally as important as faith in the Messiah was to deny the power of Christ's resurrection. For Paul, faith in Christ superseded the Torah, thereby making the detailed rules of the Torah no longer necessary. For Paul, the Torah did not bring salvation. Only Christ could—and did.

In the end, with a few compromises, Paul's position prevailed. Christianity would be built upon the life and teachings of Jesus the Christ. Except for the Ten Commandments, including love of God and neighbor, almost all the remaining moral obligations of the Torah were no longer deemed necessary.

Within a few decades, the numbers of Gentile Greek converts to Christianity quickly outnumbered the Jewish-Christian communities. This trend continued during the coming centuries. In fact, the last observant Jewish-Christian congregation on record ceased operations around the year 120 CE.

However, all Christians continued to reference the Hebrew Bible (more frequently in its Greek version known as the Septuagint). They included the "Old Testament" as part of their tradition, because they discovered in its books hints and intimations of the Messiah, or Christ, reflected in the life of Jesus of Nazareth.[2] Christians also continued to use some of the ethical and moral principles found in Hebrew wisdom literature as guidelines for Christian behavior. They looked to the Psalms as sacred prayers. They searched the Books of Wisdom and Proverbs to find rules for living.

Nevertheless, Christianity was something truly new. From Teilhard's perspective, Christianity was more than just a "new and improved" version of Judaism. It qualified as an evolutionary event because it was born and evolved from within an older religious tradition. Today, a similar debate is emerging between those who follow what may be called a "traditional Christianity" and those who are operating with a new consciousness, first proposed by Teilhard.

Traditional Christianity and a New Consciousness

For traditional Christians, humanity had lost favor with God by its sinfulness and had its friendship with God restored through the redemptive death of Jesus on the cross. Once again, people had access to God as well as to God's love and forgiveness. The loving relationship with God that had been lost by our first parents and all following generations was now restored. Jesus Christ had redeemed humanity. Through his sacrificial death on the cross, humanity was brought back into favor with God. After their death, people who died free of serious sin would enter heaven and live forever in God's loving presence. Thanks to the atoning sacrifice of Christ, they would enjoy a blissful eternal life in a kind of Garden of Eden, much like Adam and Eve had enjoyed at the beginning. However, this time, instead of only two inhabitants, the heavenly Eden would be filled with countless numbers of people to whom Christ's blood had brought salvation. That describes the Christian consciousness and conscience that continued for nearly two thousand years.

Today, the discoveries of modern science have radically changed our human consciousness. Scientific evidence finds no indication that the human species started in a state of perfection in a Garden of Eden and lost it by sin. Much more likely, the line that eventually produced *Homo sapiens sapiens* (the subspecies of the genus *Homo* in which modern humans are classified) evolved over a period of a few million years. Current archeological research evidence shows at least four distinct species emerging in the *Homo* line and becoming extinct before us. The last of these extinct species in the *Homo* line was the Neanderthal race.

According to archeology, the first of our modern human species lived a very primitive existence as hunter-gatherers. The first humans were born as children, not as fully formed adults as Adam and Eve supposedly were.[3]

Like St. Paul challenging the moral requirements demanded of converts by the Jerusalem Christians, Teilhard is challenging what we might call the restrictive scope of "traditional" morality. This was the morality practiced up to and during the Middle Ages; it was solidified in the documents of the Council of Trent (1545–63). Teilhard spent his entire life in a church that promoted that traditional morality. He died in 1955, some years before the Second Vatican Council (1962–65) began to open the church's windows to the modern world and its new consciousness.

Contrasts

To get better oriented to Teilhard's moral thinking, here are several contrasts that you will encounter throughout the rest of this book. They are contrasts between traditional morality and Teilhard's approach, between a traditional consciousness and an evolutionary consciousness.

First, a traditional moral theology would focus on what you should *not* do. After all, most of the Ten Commandments begin "Thou shall *not*…"

In contrast, Teilhard's moral focus is explicitly *positive*; it is concerned less with what you shouldn't do and more with what you can do and are called to do. It is all about making a positive difference with your life.

6

Second, the traditional approach is that *bad behaviors* to avoid are described quite clearly and precisely. In booklets for doing an examination of conscience, most sins are listed, categorized, and labeled.

In Teilhard's positive and dynamic morality, most sins have to do with *the good you failed to do or could have easily done but consciously chose not to.* The horizon of possible good behaviors, personal and collective, is vast.

Third, traditional morality focuses on the *past*, on bad behavior already completed. Its purpose is to facilitate having your sins forgiven and putting you right with God again. To use a financial metaphor, it's as if, by committing sin, we continually get into debt that we can't pay, and the church provides a way for you to get your debt forgiven. Sacraments like baptism, confession, and Eucharist provide an effective way of putting you back in favor with God. They enable you to erase your debt. Each time you use them, your financial account goes from negative back to zero. No debt.

In contrast, Teilhard's morality is focused on the *future*, on work for God's project that you and I haven't yet accomplished. For Teilhard, God is focused primarily on the future, on what still needs to be achieved to transform the world. Much of the positive ethical landscape is yet undefined and not yet envisioned. God is "a God of cosmic synthesis in whom we can be conscious of advancing and joining together by spiritual transformation of all the powers of matter."[4] Using the financial metaphor again, Teilhard would agree that Christ got us out of moral debt and moved humanity's account back up to zero. But he would argue that Christ is far more interested in helping us find investments that would help increase humanity's moral wealth. Financially, in Teilhard's mind, the purpose or aim of the moral life is to grow the world's account *upward* from zero.

Fourth, in traditional morality, you need an *outside judge* to identify whether your behavior is bad—and to decide how bad it is. Such a judge might be a priest in the confessional, a catechism's list of sins, or some explicit church rule, for example, about fasting or church attendance. In one sense, in this mindset you do not need to develop a conscience, since the church shapes your conscience for you. All you need to do is follow the rules. No need to ask questions.

In the new, dynamic morality, you have a personal responsibility to develop your conscience, to help it mature. It is up to you to form a reflective and responsible *inner manager* of your energy, especially your love energy. In forming a mature conscience, your inner manager would ask questions to help you discern how to direct your energy and coordinate it toward the growth and development of the Body of Christ.

Fifth, in traditional morality there is little need for self-development intellectually, emotionally, morally, and even spiritually. A traditional consciousness is sufficient. In it, behavior is prescribed, prayers at worship are prescribed, spirituality is prescribed (within options), and so on. Your job is to listen and obey—not to think, wonder, question, or challenge authority.

In an evolutionary morality, it is essential for individuals to nurture a mature moral, intellectual, emotional, and spiritual life. For how else, except by asking challenging questions, could one develop a consciousness and conscience that was sensitive to the urgings of the Holy Spirit?[5] For Teilhard, people need to learn to use their love energy in ways that release higher forms of human energy. He refers to humanity as "the technician and engineer of the spiritual energies of the world."[6]

Sixth, traditional morality, with its focus on sins of commission, remains *impersonal*. Sins are easily identifiable and objectively defined. Thus, a certain act is a sin, no matter who commits it, though there are conditions that might make a person less culpable. The rules for sin and avoiding sin are the same for everyone. One might say these rules are *impersonal*, that is, they apply equally to anyone and everyone.

In contrast, for Teilhard and his focus on accomplishing things for Christ, sins of omission of their nature are *personal and interpersonal*. There are moral opportunities uniquely yours, ones that only you can carry out. And there are tasks that you can carry out only in partnership with others. A person's ethics must not only be positive and practical, they also need to be *personal and interpersonal*. Implicit in this is the need for each person to develop an adult sense of responsibility and to become morally mature, individually and as an interpersonal being.

Seventh, in the traditional approach, the rules for identifying sinful behavior are always *clear and simple*. They define precisely how an individual can violate one or other of the Ten Commandments.

In contrast, Teilhard's rules mostly involve positive behavior, and are very *general, vague, and interpersonal*. Questions arise: How can one make rules for an individual's positive behavior if the guidelines are general, vague, and interpersonal? Or how can one gauge the value of any specific positive behavior? How can morality ever be clear and simple, since it is up to each person—and groups of people—to discern what God is calling them to?

Teilhard provides some guidelines for identifying practical, personal good behavior as well as collective behavior that promotes the evolutionary process that fosters God's project. One can find in Teilhard's essays and books principles for making decisions within such a dynamic, forward-looking morality.

However, before presenting Teilhard's basic principles and his ethical principles, it is important to clarify a few important terms.

2

Clarifications and Challenges

B EFORE EXPLORING TEILHARD'S approach to the moral life, let's first clarify some terms that will be used throughout the book. In this chapter, we look at how Teilhard defines *morality* and *ethics*, then at some *classical ethical models* and where Teilhard stands with respect to each. Next, we explore a term called "God's project," an image that provides an evolutionary perspective to Jesus's term, "the kingdom of God." It is also important to know that Teilhard sees *love* as the primary engine of evolutionary progress, and how growth in *consciousness* is central to the evolutionary process. Finally, this chapter develops Teilhard's two key concepts that encompass human experience: *activities* and *passivities*.

Morality and Ethics

The simplest rule for living an ethical or moral life is "to do good and avoid evil." Ethics and morals both relate to "right" and "wrong" conduct. Most people today do not make a big distinction between the terms *morality* and *ethics*. Teilhard, like most, did not make a clear distinction between them. In this book, the two terms are mostly used interchangeably.

For those who may wish for a simple distinction, *morality* is typically seen as an individual matter, a private or personal sense of what is right and wrong, while *ethics* is morality applied to a society or group, and what the group has decided or agreed to be right or wrong for its members. The American Medical Association has its code of ethics; the American Bar Association has its code of ethics; the American Psychological Association has its code of ethics. If you join such an association, you agree to abide by its ethical rules.

For Teilhard, principles of the moral life are not to be based on any socially agreed-upon rules of conduct. They are to be based on God's purposes in creation. Thus, for Teilhard, *ethics requires that persons develop the virtues and habits of character to fulfill God's purposes.* "Careful and reflective attention to the end or purpose of our acts is a necessary condition for any ethics, and theological ethics begins with discerning and acquiescing to the purposes of God in creation."[1]

This approach causes the reflective person inevitably to ask questions like, What does God say is the purpose of human life—and my human life in particular? As soon as we reflect on questions like this one, we realize that the moral life must be more than simply the avoidance of sin. It moves into the realm of positive action in order to make a difference.

A young man struggling with the question of his life's purpose came to Jesus. He posed his question by asking Jesus what was needed to attain eternal life (see Matt 19:16–22). Jesus replied, "You know the commandments." The young man said he had kept the commandments all his life, but he knew there had to be more to life than that. Then Jesus told him to sell all his possessions, give the money to the poor, and follow him. He was calling the man to a life of selfless service toward others. The young man walked away sad because, while he wanted more meaning in his life, he had many possessions and caring for them prevailed.

During the past two thousand years, most Christians have responded like the rich young man. Even though they may have wanted a deeper and richer moral life, they opted for the minimum requirements of morality: observing the Ten Commandments.

Ethical Models

Academically, we can compare Teilhard's ethical approach to three of the most common ethical models current among religious thinkers.[2]

The first is the *command and obey model*. In this juridical model, God or the church or your religious superior (bishop, pastor, abbot, provincial, etc.) gives you a command and you are obliged to obey. For example, God commanded Abraham to sacrifice his son Isaac, and Abraham would have obeyed—except God stopped him at the last moment.

In traditional religious life, this command and obey ethic was sometimes carried to absurd extremes. For example, if your abbot or mother superior commanded you to do something, even if the command was obviously frivolous or useless, you were obliged to do it. The superior might order you to dig a hole, then refill it, then dig it up again and refill it again. Or your superior might test your obedience by ordering you daily to water a dead plant, knowing that it was a sheer waste of time. This was often referred to as "blind obedience."

Most of the ethical rules in certain professions (doctors, lawyers, psychotherapists, etc.) are based on the command and obey model, where disobedience has its consequences. Professional ethical systems include their own "mortal" and "venial" versions of sins. A lawyer's smaller violation of an ethical rule may result in a fine or temporary suspension of a license to practice. A serious violation might result in the lawyer being disbarred, thus depriving him for life of his income as an attorney.

The second ethical model is an *individual human rights model*. This model arose when it became clear in some communities that certain rights of human dignity were being violated. Many state and federal laws have been passed to ensure the equal rights of all humans, regardless of religion, race, gender, age, weight, sexual preference, physical or mental limitations, and so on. This ethical model has sponsored a woman's right to vote and a woman's right to equal pay for equal work. This ethical model is behind the requirements that public buildings provide entrances accessible to handicapped people, such as those in wheelchairs. This model is also the root of the United Nations' Declaration on the Rights of Children. Many charitable foundations are based on the human right of everyone to food, safe water, clothing, and education. In the U.S. Constitution, the Bill of Rights is based on this ethical model, such as the right to privacy, the right to free speech, the right to bear arms, the right to practice one's religion, and so on. Most Christian churches base their objection to abortion and euthanasia using a "right to life" principle, applying it "from conception to natural death."

The third common ethical model is based on *classical natural law*. This means that individuals must act in accordance with their God-given nature, the unchangeable nature humans were given from the beginning of creation. Various forms of the Golden Rule might serve as good examples of this model: "Don't do to others what you wouldn't want them to do to you," or, more positively, "Do to others what you would like them to do to you." Another way of looking at classical natural law is to say that humans were meant to live in peace and harmony with one another. The last six of the Ten Commandments emerge from natural law fostering peaceful coexistence in society— don't kill, steal, lie, hate, or violate sacred relationships. In this model, living together in peace and harmony is a major moral objective.

If we were to approach Teilhard and ask him which of the three standard models he prefers, he would hesitate to accept any of them as fully satisfying his ethical approach. In their place, he might suggest a fourth model. For Teilhard, *any ethic must be built on the fact that everything is evolving*, that God is calling us forward to build a better world. In this world, love and unity are not only possible, they will become pervasive and enduring. Teilhard's new model is an *ethic of loving cooperation aimed at the development and transformation of the world*.[3] As Jesuit theologian Edward Vacek states, for Teilhard, "human morality must continue the evolutionary process and be open to further development."[4]

Instead of merely "getting along together," Teilhard wants humanity to "forge ahead." Vacek suggests that a good name for Teilhard's ethical model might be an *evolutionary natural law model*.[5] It takes the best of the existing models and re-envisions them from an evolutionary perspective. Although Teilhard's ethical model may appear much more complex than any of the other three models, the insight behind it, once grasped, is quite simple.[6]

God's Project

God's project is a key term that will be used throughout the book to describe what Jesus called "building the kingdom of God," and what St. Paul called "building the Body of Christ." Teilhard wanted to find a simple name for this evolutionary divine work. It should be an inviting image that everyone could grasp and want to contribute to. Teilhard never settled on a name; therefore, to choose an image that was very simple and clear, yet open to being ongoing and evolutionary, we will call it "God's project."

In his writings, Teilhard never called creation's divine love experiment God's project. We can tell he was searching for an appropriate name, yet never quite settled on one. For example, in the following sentence, Teilhard used four different vague expressions to describe what we are calling God's project. Teilhard's expressions for it are italicized here:

> ...to the preparation and service of this *great thing* whose emergence is foreshadowed. The *work now in progress* in the universe, the *mysterious final issue* in which we are collaborating, is that *"greater unit"* which must take precedence over everything, and to which everything must be sacrificed, if success is to be ours."[7]

God's project, then, is the name we will use throughout the book for what Teilhard is describing when he refers to this *great thing*, this *greater unit*, this *work now in progress*, and its *mysterious final issue* in which we are collaborating.

When you read the parables of Jesus describing the "kingdom of God" and "the kingdom of heaven," Teilhard would have you translate these expressions into "the divine work now in progress," or simply use the expression "God's project." Jesus was very clear about the ongoing nature of the divine project, when he said again and again, "The kingdom of heaven is at hand" (see Mark 1:15 and Matt 3:2; 4:7; 10:7). The divine work is already in full swing, he was telling us, but it is not yet complete. It has a future. For example, the Internet has radically changed the way humans relate.

Today's evolutionary path is continually being affected and modified by technology as well as by the individual and collective daily choices of billions of humans. Though humankind's evolutionary path is unpredictable, for Teilhard, its destination remains certain. God's project keeps moving forward.

Among the New Testament writings, Teilhard found support for his divine-project theology in many places in the writings of St. Paul.[8] Using Paul as a starting point, Teilhard developed a theological vision

14

of the evolving Cosmic Body of Christ, from which emerged his evolutionary spirituality.[9] For Teilhard, we are the living cells in this Cosmic Body. Each of us—every cell—is meant to become fully conscious of our participation in the divine nature. In that culminating evolutionary moment of fullest consciousness, this Christ Body will realize itself as the divine reality it was always meant to be.

Instead of the metaphor of cells in a body, Teilhard sometimes used the image of "fragments." For example, in Teilhard's own words, "the indefinite layers of Time and Space…show themselves to be the bosom which gathers together the separate fragments of a huge Consciousness in process of growth."[10] But these fragments keep rearranging themselves in more and more complex ways in an evolutionary drive. This living evolving system, he notes, "coils in collectively upon itself above our heads, in the direction of some sort of higher Mankind."[11]

He explains how our individual souls are not isolated but already joined and living together lovingly in one divine Spirit in the Cosmic Body. Gradually, he predicts, we will lose that familiar sense of isolation and separateness from one another. We are learning to feel the call to closer and closer relationships, ones that are more and more loving. Teilhard believes that, eventually in our consciousness, we will become aware that we are flowing together in the same direction—as all the molecules of water in a river flow together in the same direction—toward a oneness of mind and heart. This is a new planetary consciousness that Teilhard described as a "sort of higher Mankind." And the first step for humanity along this "single direction" is to develop a spirituality for *relationships*, not merely for individuals.[12]

The Basis of Evolutionary Progress

For Teilhard, the most universal and fundamental energy in the world is love. "Love is the most universal, the most tremendous and the most mysterious of the cosmic forces."[13] Like thought, love is still in full-growth mode in humanity. Not only do minds continue to grow and evolve, but hearts and spirits do as well.[14]

For Teilhard, there is continuity in evolution. It develops from fragments of elemental matter at the Big Bang uniting and reuniting, step by step, up to human relationships and society. And society will continue to grow in unity beyond the development we humans have reached so far. Evolution has a future, and we are partly responsible for shaping that future. As Teilhard writes, "From man onwards and in man, evolution has taken reflective consciousness of itself. Henceforth, it can to some degree recognize its position in the world, choose its direction, and withhold its efforts."[15] For him, the human species will continue to evolve primarily in the complexity of its relationships and the breadth and depth of its consciousness.

"The transition from the [love of] individuals to [love of] the collective is the present crucial problem confronting human energy."[16] Learning how to love in dyads and larger groups is the present work of people on our planet. "The unity of the evolutionary front remains intact," writes Teilhard, "and the value of the world continues to be built up ahead *by a communal effort*."[17]

For Teilhard, the true function of religion in an evolving universe "is to sustain and spur on the progress of life."[18] Unfortunately, until now, religion has not recognized its "true function."

For example, Teilhard asks us to consider how traditional religion views the true function of marriage. Most religions have seen "the progress of life" focused almost exclusively on the union of a married couple primarily for reproduction. In this traditional approach, growth is defined simply as increasing the number of believers. In its focus on marriage merely as a context for bringing children into the world, says Teilhard, traditional religion misses tremendous potential energy of a relationship's love for transforming the mind and heart of humanity as well as the planet.

For Teilhard, the purpose of married love is not merely to generate new biological life. Rather, the marriage relationship, as a new two-person unit, must find a fuller purpose in pumping new vitality into the mind and heart of humanity (what Teilhard calls the *noosphere*). Teilhard believes that God wants us to create a "common soul of humanity." And married couples can use their love potential to help create that ever-expanding common soul.

"The organization of human energy, taken as a whole, is directed and pushes us toward the ultimate formation, over and above each personal element, of a common soul of humanity."[19] To grasp Teilhard's vision for humanity, it is most important to realize how evolution has changed everything, especially our approach to moral and ethical life.

And how love provides the driving force behind everything in God's project.

Activities and Passivities

In his book of spirituality, *The Divine Milieu*, Teilhard says that we can categorize all our experiences into two groups: *activities* and *passivities*. He shows how this simple division of life experiences is at the heart of spirituality.[20] By much the same reasoning, the same division of experiences can answer some key questions at the heart of the moral life.

Although *activities* and *passivities* are not common terms for most of us, it is worth taking the time to grasp the special meaning Teilhard assigns to each of them, for they turn out to provide an effective way to enter into Teilhard's mind as well as into his spirituality and morality.

As Teilhard defines them, *activities* are decisions and actions we consciously choose to do, while *passivities* are unchosen experiences that affect us. Passivities are the things that happen to us, whether we like them or not. For example, you and I had no say regarding the year we were born, the city and nation where we were born, who our parents were, or what their genetic strengths and weaknesses were. More generally, passivities include the effects produced in us by the behavior of others, as well as by accidents, the vagaries of weather, events happening in the rest of the world, and so on. Passivities can powerfully affect us.

For Teilhard, activities often have a clear moral component. Activities—our free choices and behaviors—can go two ways: they can be chosen either to foster progress and development for ourselves or others (*activities of growth*), or to cause weakening and harm to ourselves or others (*activities of diminishment*).

Similarly, passivities—the things that happen to us—can affect us in two ways: they can either foster our healthy development (*passivities of growth*) or weaken us and hinder growth (*passivities of diminishment*).

Let's consider each of these four branches, as they form a simple way of organizing human experience:

Activities of growth include all helpful conscious decisions and actions. Such activities can *enhance* our lives, as when we form loving relationships, learn new skills, or do kind acts.

Activities of diminishment include unhelpful conscious decisions and actions. These activities can *shrink, weaken,* and *harm* our lives, as when we tell lies, bully someone, choose to seek revenge, or violate a trust.

Passivities of growth can *foster and increase* our potential, as when we happen to be born with good health into a loving family in a free country and have special talents, say, for music or mathematics.

Passivities of diminishment can *weaken and limit* our potential, as, for example, when we happen to be born into an abusive household with illiterate parents in a war-torn country and are burdened with physical or mental disabilities.

_____ Teilhard assures us that passivities outnumber activities by about a thousand to one. In fact, passivities may do more to shape our lives and character—including our moral character—than any conscious choices we may make.

_____ A child who grows up observing parents who habitually criticize and demean others is much more likely to develop and practice similar diminishment habits than a child who grows up in an affirming and creative home. According to recent statistics, more than 80 percent of grownups that abuse their children were themselves abused as children or grew up in abusive households.

So, while some events over which we have no control help shape our lives positively from our earliest years, others can affect our emerging self in potentially negative ways, right from the start.

But what about issues of morality and ethics? How do the dynamics of activities and passivities work in this context? For Teilhard, *the moral principle is to use your activities in ways that enable your passivities to help you and others, especially in fostering God's project.*

Passivities in themselves are not sins. *We can only sin using activities*—freely chosen choices and actions—in responding to the things that happen to us. Our moral and ethical life has a lot to do with how we choose to use *activities* in responding to our *passivities*.

For example, a young man with a talent for leadership might develop it and use it in ethically positive leadership capacities (*activities of growth*). A young man brought up in a family riddled with verbal and physical abuse might participate in anger management programs and consciously raise his children in loving and caring ways (*activities of growth*).

Everyone encounters experiences that diminish them as well as experiences that support growth. No one is exempt from diminishment. We all get sick or develop disease. We all have plans that must be postponed because of a rainstorm, or we miss an important appointment because of traffic congestion. We have all had to endure sitting next to self-centered people at a dinner party. All of us have been cheated by greedy people. We have all experienced rejection by school classmates or workplace colleagues.

Much of our moral lives and ethical behaviors have been shaped—and continue to be shaped—by events in our lives over which we have little or no control (*passivities*). For example, without knowing it, from the attitudes and behavior of our parents and others around us during childhood, we unconsciously adopted and internalized their moral attitudes toward race, religion, ethnic groups, gender bias, education, political preferences, and so on. Assimilation happened without any conscious thought or choice on our part. From those around us, we learned how to love and how to hate, what to fear and whom to trust, how to fight and when to run away, how to pray and how to curse, what was acceptable behavior and what was unacceptable. We absorbed and internalized the behavior and attitudes of those around us, no matter whether we were loved and valued or were rejected and left behind.

We internalized—and perhaps even imprinted—many of our attitudes and behaviors at a most impressionable age (*passivities*). Much to our dismay, we may discover that unhelpful moral attitudes and behaviors we developed unconsciously in our early years may take a lifetime to truly change. These are *passivities of diminishment*.

Recently, in an exclusive apartment building in New York City—guarded by cameras, a doorman who checks all people as they approach, and a keyed entry system—a very tall black man stepped into the building's elevator. He was a tenant and a world-famous opera singer. He pressed the button for his floor. Just before that, a white woman also stepped into the elevator, but didn't press any button. The man assumed that both he and the woman must live on the same floor. When the elevator door on his floor opened and he got out, the woman did not follow, but pressed the button to a different floor. She had refused to reveal to him the floor she lived on while he was in the elevator, such was her innate mistrust of black men, a passivity she had developed in childhood.

Bringing about a successful change in undesirable moral and ethical patterns may also require many conscious choices on our part over many years.

With these definitions in mind, we can begin to explore Teilhard's approach to morality and ethics.

3

Eight Basic Principles of Teilhard's Thought

IN A TRADITIONAL approach, spirituality revolves around private prayer, church attendance, and various devotions or pious acts. Such spiritual practices, for the most part, are "something we do around the edges [of our daily lives] when we have time."[1] Our *real* lives are involved much more with getting educated, raising a family, earning a living, and hoping to retire one day with financial security. Around the edges of our daily lives, we say our prayers, we try to ease suffering, bind wounds, and support the poor and forgotten, at least by writing checks to charitable organizations. For many, this is a familiar picture of our spiritual life. Teilhard has a very different viewpoint on spirituality—and morality.

For Teilhard, we live in an evolving world. This is the kind of world God created. And we are, consciously or unconsciously, participants in God's plans for the successful completion of that divine project. We are meant to spend our lives on Earth to promote human evolution, individually and collectively. We are called to work together and live in the ways we were meant to live—promoting transformation, transcending ourselves, being born again and again of God's spirit, just as Jesus described to Nicodemus (see John 3:1–21). When we put on Christ's mind and eyes, we begin to see our daily lives in a new way.

For Teilhard, once we have recognized our call to participate in helping evolve the human race, the Christian vocation is "no longer merely to ease the suffering, to bind up the wounds, or to succor the weak, but through every form of effort and discovery, to urge its powers by love up to their highest term."[2] Each waking hour, each choice, and

21

each action offer opportunities to make a positive difference. Our daily lives become our spiritual practice. For many, this way of spirituality and morality will appear totally strange and new.

We cannot begin to understand Teilhard's approach to this new kind of moral life and spirituality unless we build our understanding on some basic principles of his thought. Without these basic principles, we cannot begin to grasp the revolutionary import of his ethical views, since his approach to morality and ethics flow from his basic principles. Here is a list of the eight basic principles of Teilhard's thought:

Teilhard's Basic Principles

BASIC PRINCIPLE 1: God created an evolving universe.

BASIC PRINCIPLE 2: The law governing evolution may be summarized as Attraction-Connection-Complexity-Consciousness.

BASIC PRINCIPLE 3: Bringing this evolving universe to its fulfillment is God's project as well as God's purpose for creating the universe.

BASIC PRINCIPLE 4: The task of completing God's evolutionary project requires active human cooperation.

BASIC PRINCIPLE 5: Love is the very nature of God.

BASIC PRINCIPLE 6: The universe is a love project.

BASIC PRINCIPLE 7: A planetary mind and heart (the noosphere) has arisen and is evolving.

BASIC PRINCIPLE 8: In an evolutionary world *unire* provides a better foundation of metaphysics, theology, and ethics than *esse*.

Each principle will be discussed in detail in this chapter. In the following chapter, we explore eleven Teilhardian ethical principles that arise from these eight basic principles. These ethical principles form a system presenting his approach to living a moral life in an evolving world. There are undoubtedly other principles that have been missed in both lists, but these are necessary and sufficient for developing an ethical life in the spirit of Teilhard.

In each case, the principle is presented as a short statement, along with some references to it in Teilhard's writings. Furthermore, a more traditional viewpoint is offered, so that the newness of Teilhard's approach is evident in each principle. At the end of each principle, there are suggestions for your personal moral and ethical reflection.

BASIC PRINCIPLE 1:
God Created an Evolving Universe

Evolution changes our understanding of everything because it permeates every dimension of creation.[3]

Living in the twenty-first century, it is hard to imagine that, until a little more than a few centuries ago, most people held what is called a "static" or "fixed" view of the universe. This is the universe described in the early chapters of the Book of Genesis. In the time of Jesus, this was the view most people held of creation.

The Book of Genesis implies that Earth accounts for most of God's creation: Earth was a flat, solid, and unmoving world; the sun and moon revolved around it; stars were merely sparkling heavenly lights rotating annually in an orderly fashion. This static view of creation also implied that everything was created in the beginning just as we see it today. According to that belief, nothing has ever really changed or evolved. For instance, the snow-capped Alps at the first moment of their creation looked just the way these mountains look today. The deep gorge of the Grand Canyon was created just as vacationers see it today. On the day of creation, camels, chimps, chickens, and crows looked and sounded just like they do today. Adam and Eve were the first humans, and their bodies looked and worked exactly as ours do today. All of creation appeared as a finished product, perfectly executed in six divine days.

The static view of creation was never strongly challenged until the seventeenth century, when Galileo invented the telescope. We no longer had to theorize about how the Earth orbited around the sun, we could look and see for ourselves.

In the nineteenth century, another earth-shaking discovery was made: *that all living things are products of evolution.* Only after Charles Darwin published his book *On the Evolution of Species* (1849) did people begin to realize that they might have to rethink the story of Creation in evolutionary terms. Darwin showed that living species on Earth were in a *process of change*. Moreover, in each life-form, the change process was dynamic, continually developing and unfolding. Life-forms were *evolving*.

By Teilhard's day at the turn of the twentieth century, evolutionary science was blossoming. Many scientists suspected that evolution might be happening in other domains besides biology and in the plants and birds that Darwin studied. Teilhard noted, "Evolution has in a few years invaded the whole field of our experience….This evolution is giving new value as material for our action, to the whole domain of existence…providing human aspirations (for the first time in the course of history) with an absolute direction and an absolute end."[4]

Three Important Questions

Teilhard scholar and teacher Robert Faricy points out that there are three important questions about evolution that Teilhard considers, each of which is very important to our exploration of Teilhard's moral and ethical thought.[5]

At a *first level*, Teilhard asks, *Where is evolution to be found? How pervasive is it?* This is a question about where to look for *evidence*. His answer, quoted above, is that evolution is found everywhere, at least in the sense that every new thing we see on Earth was born, that is, it came from something else. Its origin can be traced to some thing or other things that came before it. As an obvious example, today's smartphone did not just appear out of the blue. It had generations of ancestors that gave birth to it. In each new generation, it had developed new properties and abilities to adapt to the human environment. In other words, the phone evolved, and will probably continue evolving.

Near the end of the twentieth century, after Teilhard had died, a further step in our understanding of evolution was made with the mapping of the human genome and the genomes of other creatures. While Darwin, in the last line of *The Evolution of Species*, merely suspected that all living species on Earth evolved ultimately from a single cell, genomic science recently reconfirmed Darwin's conjecture. All life on Earth can be traced back to single-celled creatures in the sea, thus validating the universal evolutionary process of new life forms. Genomic mapping revealed that the human genome shared genetic similarities with almost every living thing, including fish and worms. We now know that our planet is one totally interdependent biosocial evolving creation.[6] In this very basic sense, everything that exists today evolved over time into its present state. This evidence-level of evolution is the focus of Teilhard's first basic principle.

At a *second level*, the evolutionary question Teilhard faced was, *Is there a consistent process by which evolution works—by which new things, especially living things, are born? Is there a law governing evolution?* This is a question of *process*. Teilhard's discovery of evolution's process may be formulated in what he calls the "law of complexity-consciousness." The workings of this law and its development is explained in Teilhard's second basic principle.

At a *third level*, the evolutionary question Teilhard faced was, *Does evolution have a direction? Is it moving toward something discernible or identifiable?* This is a question of evolution's *purpose or meaning*. Teilhard answers this question in the affirmative. His exploration of evolution's purpose is discussed in his third basic principle and more fully developed in the basic principles that follow it.

A Universal Process

The biblical stories of Creation are so ingrained in our collective cultural and religious psyches that it is difficult for many people of faith to acknowledge that creation might *not* have happened exactly as the Hebrew Scriptures tell it. Those who adhere to the literal interpretation of the Genesis story of Creation—and there are many—simply deny evolution.[7] Teilhard, however, is unequivocal.

Evolution is not merely a theory or a hypothesis, he says, *but the most universal process happening on Earth—and throughout the universe.* "Evolution is a general condition, which all theories, all hypotheses, all systems must submit to and satisfy from now on in order to be conceivable and true."[8] Evolution is not merely a major force of biological life, it is the underlying and defining force operating at all levels of being and life.[9] So, evolution impacts everything, even our theology, spirituality, and moral life.

Transformations and developments driven by evolution continue to happen on all levels of existence. Such advances continue to emerge in communication, transportation, technology, media, commerce, farming, ecology, politics, medicine, mathematics, physics, chemistry, anthropology, psychology, and so on. Evolution has changed every-thing we thought we knew about us and our purpose on Earth. For this reason, evolution has also affected morality and ethics.

Since life continues to evolve, evidence suggests that *God, from the beginning, must have had an evolutionary plan or project.* For Teilhard, this divine process in which we humans are totally immersed has a purpose, a direction, and a goal. And we humans are not mere onlookers, but people called to play a role in that process. Therefore, God's splendid work and its continued progress stand at the forefront of the considerations of moral theology. We are morally committed to help create the future. There is a force within us driving that commitment. It is what Teilhard scholar Ilia Delio calls the "power of attraction toward what lies ahead."

Completion of God's project becomes the primary moral challenge. Rather than remaining focused on sin and redemption, Teilhard might say, the moral task for each of us today is to make our contribution to helping further the evolutionary project that God began almost four-teen billion years ago. For Teilhard, "Evolution is not background to the human story; it *is* the human story."[10]

What science assures us is that what we call a "messy" world is simply how evolution works. Until very recently, most religious people believed that God's "perfect" universe was originally spoiled by a sin-ful act of the first pair of humans. In fact, astrophysicists tell us, the universe has been very messy, dangerous, and destructive since the Big Bang, many billions of years before the first humans appeared on our planet. For example, in larger galaxies, planets and meteors collide. Stars eat away at nebulae. On Earth, nature sometimes acts wickedly with its storms, tornados, hurricanes, earthquakes, eruptions, tsunamis, droughts, frosts, and floods. Bugs, birds, and beasts, all striving to sur-vive, multiply, and operate in the same restricted areas: they adapt to survive or go extinct. Integral to evolution is birth, suffering, death, and new life. Growth and development on Earth has always been a messy process. People have accidents, they get sick, they play in dangerous places. It has always been so.

The evolutionary process naturally involves trial and error. Mistakes are frequent, accidents are common. Each life form never ceases to try to adapt to its surroundings by a kind of "groping" or inventing or using each chance opportunity to make some progress.[11] There are millions of life-forms on land and in the seas, and millions of individuals of each form. All are struggling to find food and survive. In the food chain, many animal species eat other living species as food. In summary, all forms of sentient life—from plants and flowers, to insects and bacteria, to our pets and our loved ones—experience suffering, pain, and death.

All creation has experienced these natural diminishments—suffering, death, disasters—billions of years before *Homo sapiens* emerged on the planet. It is a scientific fact that, long before humans arrived, animal species experienced suffering, pain, death, and even extinction. Moreover, reptiles, birds, mammals, and all the rest of the animal world commonly manifested "evil" behaviors that we associate with the seven capital (or deadly) sins. Long before humans appeared, animals were demonstrating anger, greed, pride, envy, lust, gluttony, and laziness. Humans didn't invent the seven deadly sources of sin, we merely gave them names.

The process of birth and death is a fundamental law of development.[12] We are all familiar with birth and death. It happens continuously all around us. It happens to the flowers in our gardens, with our pets, and with loved ones. Death did not first appear after Adam and Eve sinned in the Garden of Eden. For billions of years before the first humans walked the earth, birth and death were happening everywhere in the universe, including Earth. In the heavens, old stars were burning out and new stars were being born. On Earth, every thing and every creature had its lifespan, and each was born from something or someone else. Physical evolution would be impossible without the process of birth and death. Metaphorically, the same is true of intellectual evolution and spiritual evolution. Older ideas die and are replaced by more comprehensive ones. Our understanding of the meaning of spiritual growth has continually evolved. Spiritual practices, such as self-inflicted bodily pain, that didn't really produce spiritual growth died off and newer, healthier ones developed in their place.

We resist death yet dream that our children and grandchildren will live in a better world than we knew. God planted that dream for progress and development into our bodies and souls. We are hardwired to be of service to others.

Evolution usually moves slowly but is moving more quickly in certain areas. Human dwellings have evolved from cave living to modern homes with all their conveniences and comforts. We didn't do it in a year—or even a century. It took thousands of years.

Churches are among the institutions that tend to evolve very slowly. Yet sometimes they take a leap forward. No one expected the evolutionary "leap" that the Catholic Church made with its ecumenical council that we call Vatican II. That event thrust a medieval-thinking church into the modern world.

Since the documents of Vatican II, published in the mid-1960s, were all written before there were any favorable papal pronouncements on evolution, one looks in vain for any explicit mention of evolution in any of its documents.[13] However, the "spirit of evolution" was clearly in the air during that ecumenical council.[14] For example, the document *Gaudium et Spes* (Pastoral Constitution on the Church in the Modern World) states,

> May the faithful, therefore, live in very close union with the other men of their time and may they strive to understand perfectly their way of thinking and judging, as expressed in their culture. Let them blend new sciences and theories and the understanding of the most recent discoveries with Christian morality and the teaching of Christian doctrine, so that their religious culture and morality may keep pace with scientific knowledge and with the constantly progressing technology. Thus they will be able to interpret and evaluate all things in a truly Christian spirit.[15]

Teilhard would have applauded that paragraph!

Sometimes, the evolutionary process moves faster, and change happens in less than a century. In the early twentieth century, there was much resistance to people giving up travel by riding horses and buggies and being forced to drive motorcars. During that transition, companies that produced horsewhips and blacksmiths who hammered out horseshoes had to go out of business to make room for automakers and auto repair shops. Horse traders became used car salesmen. Blacksmiths became auto mechanics.

Sometimes, evolution moves very fast. Consider how quickly people shifted from a stationary home telephone to the mobile phone. The next shift from the mobile phone to a slim smartphone, carried in a purse or pocket, took less than a decade. Everywhere you look you see evolution happening.

While evolution sometimes has its ups and downs, the moving picture over long periods of time shows progress. Things, as Teilhard says, are moving forward and upward.[16] The moment you think everything new has been invented, you are surprised to find yourself surrounded by dozens of new contraptions. Human nature is essentially creative and always searching for something new and/or improved. That is how the Creator made us. If you read Genesis 1, the *only thing God does for the first six days is create*—bringing into existence something that didn't exist before. On the sixth day, God creates humans "in God's own image and likeness." But the only thing we know about God's "likeness" is that God is a creative being. And, therefore, so are we.

The Evidence

To see evolution's effects on our lives, one has only to observe how far humanity has come in just the last thirty thousand years—in knowledge, technology, energy, communication, transportation, medicine, education, information storage, social life, and other areas. Advancements in each of these fields pose moral questions.

For example, tremendous advances in electronic information storage and information access raise ethical issues of privacy. Computer search engines today, sweeping through data about you in social media sites, financial transactions, and corporate information, can assemble facts about you, your life, your activities, your financial status, your work, your family, and so on. When assembled, these disparate facts create a very revealing (and perhaps somewhat embarrassing) portrait of you. Computers can be programmed to do such a search, whether you agree or not. Or your privacy may be invaded more directly by computer hacking.

In medicine, certain advances have moral and ethical implications. Many of these advances have happened since Teilhard died. We can now prolong human life almost indefinitely for those in a coma or vegetative state. We can now fertilize human eggs in vitro. We can edit the very DNA and RNA of plants, insects, birds, animals, and even humans. We have medications that can control a woman's ovulation cycle. We can implant computer chips in a human brain. We can transplant vital organs from one body to another. We can keep a faulty heart beating with a pacemaker—for a lifetime. I have a friend who has been kept alive for over sixty years by a series of pacemakers, each one replaced after eight or ten years. There are many thousands walking around and going about their daily lives with mechanical knees and hips, robotic arms and legs, cochlear implants, and many other devices that have been developed since Teilhard's time.

Evolution, Teilhard points out, is the "single fundamental current" flowing through all reality and unifying all domains of human knowledge and development. Evolution is the one constant driving force in all creation. It is God-given. For Teilhard, evolution is God's secret formula that will help bring about the reign of God on Earth.

Naturally Evolutionary

Reflecting on your own experience, you will observe that we all think naturally in evolutionary terms. However, we normally don't notice or realize it. For example, whenever you make plans—long- or short-term—you are typically envisioning a future that is different from and better than the present. That is the essence of evolutionary thinking. You schedule a vacation for yourself or others because you hope to return home afterward refreshed and invigorated, better than before. Or, you have an insight at your workplace on how to improve some process or procedure. Or, you prepare to go back to college to develop new learning and new skills. Or, you arrange with a contractor to make certain improvements in your home. Or, you invite a group together to start a book discussion group. Or, you give a donation to a Native American reservation school in hope that some young people there may grow up to become engineers or scientists. Or, you contribute to a charity doing Alzheimer's research.

Did you start a college tuition fund for your child or grandchild? Did you agree to take a job where you knew you could make a positive contribution? Did you volunteer to coach a Little League team? In every case, your intent was to change and improve the future. In each case, you were initiating an evolutionary process that you hoped would make a better world.

Teilhard says that our innate desire to create evolutionary progress shows that God did not create a perfect world, but a perfectible one. You know that fact. You live it out every day. You are not perfect, but you know you can improve.

For example, your child begins violin lessons. The first sounds she makes on the violin may sound like a screeching cat. However, a month later, with daily practice encouraged by you, she is confidently playing a simple melody that you recognize. In a few years, she will be performing in the school orchestra.

Remember your first day in algebra class or geometry class? You were sure you would never learn how to solve an equation or prove a theorem. Yet, with daily practice and faithfully doing homework, it began to get easier even though the problems got harder. Life is a process of continual improvement and eventual mastery. These are all ordinary stages in the evolutionary process. We imagine what is possible, then proceed to make it happen.

Do not be tempted to think of evolution as if it were some kind of cosmic process going on outside yourself, or as if it were the title of a college philosophy course to which you were assigned, or some mystery you were meant to study and analyze prayerfully. Teilhard wants us to recognize that evolution is happening at every moment in each of us and around us, individually and collectively. Every day of our lives, we are immersed in the whole divine process.

Teilhard would even say that now that we have become conscious of evolutionary processes all around us, we have become responsible, with God, for the progress and success of God's evolutionary project. Although the process was divinely initiated by God and is continually guided by God, God has now put awareness of this process into our minds—and hands. And God is asking us, What are you going to do about it? Are you going to join me?

The discovery of evolution presents a major challenge to Christian ethics because it alters our understanding of human life, its origins, its meaning, our collective purpose, and the life purpose of each person.

This first basic principle is foundational for a contemporary morality and ethics that emerges from Teilhard's thought.

Next, look at some simple actions and choices you have made recently—or even earlier today—that you did because you hoped for a positive outcome. For example, you complimented someone at work. Realize that you gave that affirmation to acknowledge that they are a person worthy of respect. We live in the spirit of evolution every day.

BASIC PRINCIPLE 2:
The Law Governing Evolution

This principle can be summarized as Attraction-Connection-Complexity-Consciousness.

Once we acknowledge the overwhelming evidence for evolution, Teilhard says, we must look for what guides or governs its movement. Is there a clear process occurring? Are there patterns that manage its advance and direct its path? Are there evolutionary rules or laws that can be identified?

Teilhard was interested not merely in getting people—especially people of faith—to acknowledge the universality of evolution or even to accept it passively or willingly tolerate it. He wanted to evoke a much more active response. He wanted to show people how to keep evolving. He wanted them to *practice* evolving in their daily lives. He wanted them to live an evolutive life.

Many of the evolutionary processes going on in nature appear to be governed by seemingly random activity, natural selection, artificial selection, symbiosis, and other forms of change. Many scientists see evolution as a totally random event. However, Teilhard noticed that, despite the apparent randomness and ups and downs of evolution, there also appears to be an underlying law governing evolution. He needed to uncover a basic law that governs how evolution works. This law may be observed over extended periods. It is not a measure of space or distance. It is not a measure of time. It is a measure of growing complexity. Complexity is the measurement Teilhard discovered that would reveal evolution's law.

He believed that if we knew how to apply this basic law, we could better cooperate with God in transforming our world, our small part of the kingdom of God. Using this law, we could more consciously fulfill our promise to God when we say, "Thy kingdom come. Thy will be done on Earth."

Teilhard succeeded admirably in his quest to identify the law governing and guiding evolution. His original version of this law was the *Law of Complexity-Consciousness*.[17] Some would consider his discovery of the Law of Complexity-Consciousness driving evolution the equivalent of Isaac Newton's discovery of the laws of gravity.

Eight Basic Principles of Teilhard's Thought

A more complete four-stage version of Teilhard's evolutionary law may be stated as the *Law of Attraction-Connection-Complexity-Consciousness*.[18] Once you grasp the meaning of these four stages, you will realize how familiar this evolutionary law is to almost everyone.

This is how the evolutionary law works. It begins with Attraction. Attraction leads to Connection. This movement from Attraction to Connection describes the familiar process we use to form friendships, families, partnerships, teams, communities, and all other forms of inter-personal unions and connections—all of which we trust will lead to a better life. We find ourselves attracted to someone or something—or someone finds us attractive—and we make a Connection.[19]

If you haven't noticed before, these Connections—friendships, families, teams, and so on—enjoy a life of their own. We value these Connections as crucial elements of our lives. As individual persons, we are enhanced by our Connections, challenged by them, and discover traits, talents, and abilities in ourselves that we might otherwise never have developed, if it were not for those Connections.[20] Teilhard also came to realize that his evolutionary law is in fact a law of love, because it explains the way love operates. Love begins essentially with Attraction and leads to Connection.

As part of the Connection stage, Teilhard discovered another evolutionary law, which he summarized in two words: "Union differentiates." (*Union* is the French word for "connection.") Teilhard observed that connections, relationships, and teams, as a rule, have more potential to make a difference than individuals by themselves.

Moreover, he realized that healthy unions or relationships can transform the people who are partners in them. A common misunderstanding suggests that in deep relationships people's individual personalities are lost or that they tend to blend and lose their individuality. The reality is quite the opposite. Teilhard points out that healthy relationships reveal qualities in each partner that were never noticed before. Connections "differentiate" the people who live within them. An obvious inference from this is that healthy relationships not only enable partners to behave and act in new and creative ways, but they also help build, shape, and more fully reveal each partner's personality and character. In a word, healthy relationships can make you a better person, an enriched person, and a more whole person.

We all have relationships that have brought out the best in us. Such Connections typically lead to a better life for us and for others.

Connection is a true evolutionary stage with its own emergent properties. In other words, it is precisely in a relationship where the fullness of personality and individual capacities emerge. One does not lose oneself in a relationship, but it is in relationship where one truly finds oneself.

Complexity and Consciousness

Connections lead to the next evolutionary stage—Complexity. Whether we like it or not, Connections inevitably bring Complexity into our lives.[21] Think, for example, of a newly married couple learning to live together, or a person starting work at a new job at a large office or initiating a new friendship. Each new Connection or relationship forces us to deal with new personalities, new demands on our time, new responsibilities as well as the interpersonal conflicts and confusion that arise, which call for broader understanding and forgiveness. We learn to make allowances and compromises to preserve the Connections we value. This is the experience of Complexity. We accept the challenges posed by Complexity because we trust they will lead to a better life for us and for others.

Complexity is not the same as "complication" or "confusion." Nor is Complexity merely a sheer multiplicity of elements. When Teilhard uses the term *Complexity*, he is referring to an *organized multiplicity of elements*. This organized multiplicity is usually arranged around a person or a purpose. For example, a family is not merely a multiplicity of human beings, but an organized human system whose purpose is mutual care. Similarly, a sports team is not merely a multiplicity of players but an organized system of players and strategy, whose purpose is playing a certain sport.

"Confusion" and "complications" may arise in the early process of organizing growing Complexity. For example, when the first baby is born, or an athlete first joins a team, the parents and team members face both confusion and complications: new needs arise, personality adjustments must be made, use of time must be rearranged, and new responsibilities need to be accepted. As roles and assignments are gradually clarified, confusion subsides and complications are reduced. But the Complexity remains, and its demands continue.

A new level of Complexity normally requires developing a new level of Consciousness. A new perspective is the only way to adequately grasp and manage the new multiplicity of questions, issues, and challenges. For example, new parents need to learn how to care for the baby as well as to continue to care for each other. The athlete needs to get to know the personalities of the other players as well as adapt to the coach's strategy and memorize the team playbook.

To make sense of each new element of Complexity and integrate it into our lives and loves, we stretch our Consciousness to make it more all-embracing, more understanding. We begin to manifest this new Consciousness in our choices and actions. We no longer think merely of ourselves—our wishes and wants. Our hearts and minds reach new levels of awareness. Likewise, our actions stretch beyond our self-focused boundaries and reach more encompassing levels. We begin considering—then serving—the needs of others, of family members, friends, teammates, colleagues at work, neighbors, the unemployed, the needs of our city, our nation, and the world.

As our Consciousness expands to include more and more people, it grows to be more and more like the loving, all-embracing consciousness of God. This expansion of Consciousness to become more and more all-embracing is a process that Teilhard calls "spiritualization." We notice that, while some people may stay locked up in their personal lives and interests, many others with wider interests are becoming "spiritualized."

As Teilhard writes, "We are spiritualized by being carried along by the spiritualization of all things. We are united to Christ by entering into communion with all men. We will be 'saved' [made whole] by an option that has chosen the whole."[22]

Teilhard calls us to develop what he calls "a sense of the human." It is the realization that our Consciousness is meant to embrace everyone. As a human family in this new century, we are indeed on the road to reaching "a sense of the human," but we still have a long way to go.[23]

It is important to recognize that there are many who have evolved in Consciousness and already have developed "a sense of the human." Think of the thousands who work with Doctors Without Borders, The Heifer Project, Oxfam, the World Health Organization. These are people who see all humans as part of the human family. They are members of the world household who need to be fed, housed, educated, and cared for medically. Consciousness is awareness plus appropriate response.

It is important to consider this evolutionary law of Attraction-Connection-Complexity-Consciousness from an ethical and moral perspective. In this book, we consider how this four-stage law (1) pervades existence in general, and (2) affects our moral and ethical lives. We want to begin asking ourselves questions, such as, "How do I make moral and ethical decisions using the law of Attraction-Connection-Complexity-Consciousness?" "How can I help the Connections I belong to use this evolutionary law?"

Using the Evolutionary Law

To live with an evolutionary mindset in making ethical decisions, we can use the four-stage law of evolution. Namely, we promote Attraction, Connection, Complexity, and Consciousness wherever we can—in our personal lives, our families, our friendships, our daily work, our commitments, and so on. To summarize:

- God created an evolving universe.
- Bringing creation to its evolutionary fulfillment is God's divine project.
- To accomplish it, God is always at work in and with creation using the evolutionary law.
- God's purpose and aim for creation—the goal of the divine project—is the fullest conscious loving union of all creation.
- God embedded the law of Attraction-Connection-Complexity-Consciousness in every subatomic particle at the moment of Creation (the Big Bang).
- From the beginning, this law has been operating in and driving everything in creation, especially humans, toward the completion of God's project.
- Evolution is happening continually on all levels of being.
- Evolution follows a direction guided by the Law of Attraction-Connection-Complexity-Consciousness.
- This law explains the how and why of evolution as it has been happening on all levels.
- This law also predicts and guides creation (as an inner driver) toward its fullest loving conscious union.

- Knowing this evolutionary law and how it works enables us to cooperate more effectively with what God is doing in the world.
- The evolutionary law works spirally, that is, in each cycle, it repeats its attractive force at ever higher levels.

Therefore, in a new relationship, you may first be attracted to form a connection because of the other's personal appearance or physical beauty. In a further cycle of the evolutionary law, you may then discover the other's sense of humor and develop a connection based on shared laughter. In a higher cycle, you may discover the other's compassion toward the needy and develop a connection to serve the poor. In a still higher cycle, you may discover the other's desire to discern his or her life's purpose and feel a desire to do your own discernment. During each cycle of the evolutionary law—Attraction-Connection-Complexity-Consciousness—you are challenged to evolve, again and again, personally and in your relationship.

Teilhard calls this repeated application of the four-stage evolutionary law "the law of recurrence."[24] In other words, these four stages produce their evolutionary effects over and over, not only in you and me, but in all things endlessly throughout the ages of Earth and the eons of the universe.[25]

Humans are continually affecting the evolutionary process—positively and negatively. For Teilhard, God's project cannot be completed without the conscious moral and ethical cooperation and creative efforts of humanity. God wants and needs humans to cooperate in the divine project, that is, to help fulfill the purpose and aim of creation.

Your true life's purpose is to be an instrument of God's work in the world. Therefore, your moral task is to develop your talents and capacities to better contribute to that part of the divine work that only you can uniquely do in your time and place. Teilhard has identified the law of Attraction-Connection-Complexity-Consciousness so that we can more confidently fulfill that moral task.

This leads us to ask, Why would God create an evolving universe, rather than one where everything was perfect from the start?

Basic Principle 3:
God's Purpose for Creating the Universe

Bringing this evolving universe to its fulfillment is God's project as well as God's purpose for creating the universe.

Evolution is best observed over extended periods of time and in light of the four-stage law of evolution. When believers do this, God's grand plan or project becomes clear. Why else would God create an evolving universe? Why else would God need almost 14 billion years to ultimately produce a planet that finally gave birth to human beings? God wanted to involve us consciously in that grand project, especially when humans seem naturally driven to create, innovate, discover, make progress, build new unities, and improve their lives and their world.

Traditionally, Christians believed that God's purpose for creating the world was as a testing ground for humans. After a lifetime on Earth, each person would be judged or evaluated at death as worthy—or not—to enter heaven. In that traditional theological framework, one's specific contributions to society or science were of little importance. What was important was how well you did on the ultimate "test," how caringly you lived your life and how successfully you avoided sin. In this traditional approach, you lived *on* Earth, but were not *of* it. You were merely a temporary visitor.

From this moral traditional perspective, there would be little reason for a person to put effort into improving human life on Earth. Moreover, for many centuries, most human effort was spent on just getting through life. Consequently, believers were counseled to stay focused on making sure they died in the state of grace, so they would get to enjoy "eternal rest" in heaven.[26]

In contrast, observing the process of evolution happening everywhere on Earth, Teilhard saw God's purpose for creation in a different light. For Teilhard, God's purpose in creating—the universe in general, and humanity in particular—was *not* to set up a test-for-heaven system, or even to see if people could avoid temptations to sin, or to make humans feel guilty, evil, worthless, and fearful of God's wrath.

Rather, God's purpose is to have us spend our lives on Earth helping one another—and God—make our "perfectible" planet an ever-better place to live. In other words, God wants us to spend our lifetime finding ways to love one another more deeply so that our planet would eventually become covered with people loving one another. Teilhard saw many ways of showing love, ways that might not immediately spring to mind. His ways to show love for one another might involve, as examples, using new technology, making new scientific discoveries, engaging in new psychological research, uncovering new knowledge, developing new ways of relating, and so on.

Without our cooperative effort, God not only will not but *cannot* bring about "Thy kingdom come. Thy will be done on Earth."

In the sixteenth century, St. Teresa of Avila (1515–82) grasped St. Paul's image of humans as representing parts of Christ's body (see 1 Cor 12:12–31) in her poem *Christ Has No Body*.

> Christ has no body now but yours,
> No hands, no feet on Earth but yours.
> Yours are the eyes with which he looks compassionately on
>   the world.
> Yours are the feet in which he walks to do good.
> Yours are the hands with which he blesses the world.
> Yours are the hands,
> Yours are the feet,
> Yours are the eyes.
> You are his body.
> Christ has no body now on Earth but yours.

St. Teresa's point is that creaturely activity can be done only by creatures and not by God independently of those creatures. The moral insight is that human cooperation and commitment is necessary for the building of the world. A house cannot be built without masons, plumbers, carpenters, electricians, painters, and so on. The Earth cannot be transformed without human beings each doing their part of the work for God's project. From Teilhard's perspective, God cannot accomplish what God wants to accomplish without our cooperation.[27] God counts on our dreams, our longings, our creativity, and our determination in figuring out how to build the Earth.[28] More directly, for Teilhard, *the will of God is a project to be cocreated with God through the exercise of our own minds, hearts, and bodies.*

39

As part of God's project, it seems clear that every human person during his or her lifetime on Earth has the ability and unique opportunities to contribute in one or more ways to the divine project.

Here is a powerful example of human advancement in which Teilhard would have delighted. For a long time, optical microscopy was held back by a presumed limitation. In 1873, Ernst Abbe, an expert in microscopes, stipulated a physical limit for the maximum resolution in a traditional microscope. Abbe said microscopes could never reveal anything smaller than 0.2 micrometers.

"Impossible!" he decreed. "It can't be done!"

We've all heard those words. Regardless of our field of interest, we have heard professors and colleagues, often of the highest rank and esteem, make comments about the impossibility of accomplishing this or achieving that.

So, for a hundred years, no one ever tried to prove Ernst Abbe wrong. Everyone believed that the field we now commonly call nanoscopy[29] was impossible. Then, some brave folks tried, and succeeded.

What happened was that, instead of continuing to say, "It can't be done," a few daring chemists said, "Let's find a way." And they did.

Helped by fluorescent molecules, each of three chemists, Eric Betzig, Stefan W. Hell, and William E. Moerner, found diverse ways that, when combined, would ingeniously circumvent this limitation. In 2014, many years after their discovery, they were awarded the Nobel Prize in Chemistry. Thanks to their groundbreaking work, the optical microscope can now peer into the nanoworld. They opened a field that is known as nanoscopy. Today, nanoscopy is used worldwide. As a result, new knowledge of great benefit to humanity is produced daily.[30]

For example, scientists can now visualize the pathways of individual molecules inside living cells. They can see how molecules create synapses between nerve cells in the brain. They can track aggregating proteins involved in Parkinson's, Alzheimer's, and Huntington's diseases. They can follow individual proteins in fertilized eggs as they divide into embryos. They can facilitate DNA editing. All because some people said, "Maybe it's *not* impossible."

Divine Creation was not finished in seven days, as Genesis suggests. God's project for creation will find its fulfillment only in the conscious, creative loving union of all humanity in Christ. Creation is an ongoing event. It is still a divine project in process. It is being driven by the law of Attraction-Connection-Complexity-Consciousness. Thanks to this law, creation is evolving with a definite direction and purpose toward which God is attracting it. God is focused on the future, on what still needs to be achieved. For Teilhard, creation is maturing within a divine milieu. It is maturing within the universal or Cosmic Christ.[31]

Theologically speaking, *God's project is bringing to fulfillment a Person*, whom Teilhard called the Cosmic Christ. As St. Paul put it, we live and move and have our being in that divine Person. We humans, as a species, are maturing within this divine milieu called the Cosmic or universal Christ.[32]

Teilhard calls this process of creation's loving maturation in Christ *Christogenesis*. That is, Christ is still in the process of becoming the universal being he was meant to be. Christ has not yet reached his fullest potential, because his Body, the human family, is still developing, growing, maturing.

For St. Paul, the Body of Christ is a Cosmic Body, of which we humans are a part. That universal Body is still incomplete, still immature, still becoming what it is meant to be, still in process. For St. Paul and Teilhard, it is Christ's Body that is continually being perfected (see Eph 4:11–13).[33] Bringing that divine Body to its fulfillment is God's project. *Christogenesis* is the most important project happening in the universe. It is an evolutionary project.

From this perspective, obedience to the Ten Commandments becomes merely a small part of a much larger, lifetime moral commitment to building the Earth toward the loving unity that God envisions for it. Instead of focusing on avoiding "sins of commission," Teilhard focuses much more on "sins of omission," those activities that we could be doing but are not doing that would keep the evolutionary process moving forward and upward toward God's vision for us all.

Christ has not yet reached his fullest potential. For someone to reject the divinely initiated evolutionary process, so obviously at work in every area of life, would be to reject God's will. "Thy will be done on Earth." But what is that divine "will" for us, individually and collectively?

A Happy Coincidence

In visiting a friend's home for dinner, I had occasion to use the so-called powder room. On its wall in artistic script hung a quotation from

_____ Martin Luther. As I read the words of the founder of Protestantism, I was struck by their evolutionary flavor. Luther seemed to understand God's project. I stayed long enough in that powder room to copy the Luther quote:

_____ This life, therefore, is not righteousness
But growth in righteousness,
Not health but healing,
Not being but becoming,
Not rest but exercise.
We are not yet what we shall be,
But we are growing toward it.
The process is not yet finished
But it is going on.
This is not the end but it is the road.
All does not yet gleam in glory,
But all is being purified.[34]

Christ is building and transforming Earth and everything on it, and we are God's partners in this magnificent work—God's project. This relationship to Christ is a moral and spiritual one, but it is also a scientific, educational, political, social, and aesthetic one.

Basic Principle 4:
God Requires Active Human Cooperation

The task of completing God's evolutionary project requires active human cooperation.

Traditionally, it was believed that humans could add nothing to God, since God was perfect and already complete in every way. God was almighty, all-knowing, all-seeing—total perfection. Moreover, everything that God created had to be perfect. In that traditional picture of creation, God could not create anything that was imperfect. When we discovered that nature and people were pretty messed up, we decided that it couldn't be God's fault. It had to be humans who marred God's perfect creation.

But now that we have come to realize that God created an evolving universe and that this universe still has a long way to go before it becomes "perfect." The picture has changed. Teilhard realized that currently in the evolutionary process on Earth, humanity still had much evolving to do before it fully matures. One might say that the human race is still in an early adolescent phase of growth. For some, the evidence suggests we are still toddlers. We are confused about our decisions. At times, we are overconfident. We make mistakes. We overestimate our abilities. We're impatient. We compare ourselves to others. We want what others have. Our brains fixate on recent events and blow them out of proportion. In other words, humanity hasn't yet developed to its fullest potential.[35] The following story is a good example of our current immaturity by a workshop leader who understood it:

> A group of 500 people were attending a seminar on teamwork. As a group activity, the speaker asked his helpers to hand each person a balloon and a marker pen. Each person was to write their name on their balloon. The 500 balloons were collected and put in another room.
>
> The people were then led into that room. They were given five minutes to find the balloon with their name on it. Everyone began frantically searching for their balloon, pushing people aside, colliding with each other. It was utter chaos. At the end of 5 minutes practically no one had found their own balloon.
>
> Then, the speaker asked each person to pick up any balloon and give it to the person whose name was written on it. Within minutes everyone had their own balloon.
>
> The speaker explained, "This chaos is happening in our lives. Everyone is frantically searching for happiness all around, not knowing where it is. Our true purpose lies in fostering the happiness of others. Give them their happiness. Others will bring you your own happiness. This is the purpose of human life, to work together in the pursuit of happiness.

God is trying to bring all things into fulfillment in Christ and help us to mature. To do this, God needs conscious, active, and mature human cooperation. God wants us to go forth and make a difference.[36]

We were put on Earth for a divine purpose, not just to "wait, watch, and pray."

When you look at the lives of the saints, they were aware of the need for action to help make the world a better place. St. Francis of Assisi felt that God was calling him to "rebuild the church." St. Ignatius Loyola felt called to renew and refurbish the church's educational system and reinvigorate the faithful, so his Jesuits created schools, colleges, and universities. St. Vincent de Paul felt a call to serve the poor and founded active religious congregations to help him. Even the cloistered contemplative St. Thérèse of Lisieux focused the intentions of her prayers and her energy spent in suffering toward the success of foreign missionary work. All of us—not merely the saints—are called to be intimately involved in helping complete God's project. Action is called for. With this new perspective of God's project, Christians are learning to see everything in this world in its divine depths. We are recognizing its tremendous potentials.[37]

We are urged by Teilhard to participate actively in the process of *Christogenesis*. For him, it is morally imperative to help in every way to bring about the maturation of the human family, to share in its searching, its hopes, its accomplishments.[38] In a very real sense, with God's help, we humans—in the decisions we make—are mainly responsible for the future of humanity and the planet.

Teilhard envisions a revolution in morality and ethics, which is like the Copernican revolution in astronomy. Instead of a morality that revolves primarily around the safety, security, and salvation of the self, it becomes a morality that revolves primarily around what each person, in cooperation with others, can do to foster what God is doing in transforming our world. In this new perspective, one's life purpose becomes so much larger and part of a much grander plan than one's own personal salvation. Each one's life purpose becomes the safety, security, and success of the whole divine project.[39]

For many centuries, we have recited the Lord's Prayer, saying, "Thy will be done on Earth," thinking that God's will meant only that we should stay out of sin and be kind to our neighbor. Considering God's grand evolutionary project, envisioned by Jesus, especially in John's Gospel, and for St. Paul, God's will for us on Earth has a much larger purpose. We are to be focused, not primarily on avoiding sin, but rather on spending our years on Earth helping to foster and complete

God's evolutionary project. Teilhard might say that we are meant to be cocreators of the future.

We desire to promote and help accomplish God's project, since accomplishing this divine project is also God's desire. For you to show your deepest love for God is to want to accomplish with all your heart what God desires. God is delighted by our loving cooperation in the divine project.[40]

Frank Sheed and Masie Ward met as Catholic activists and street-corner preachers in London in the early years of the twentieth century. In 1926, they founded Sheed & Ward Publishing Company. It was their attempt to try something for God that they believed would fill an important spiritual gap in religious publishing. On one end of the spectrum, there were plenty of Catholic publishers in England that printed Bibles, prayer books, and catechisms. On the other end, there were those who provided textbooks for Catholic seminarians. However, there was no publisher printing religious books for educated Catholic laypeople. That's where Sheed & Ward chose to make their spiritual impact.

Sheed & Ward provided serious biographies of saints and other notables, as well as books on theology that went beyond grammar school catechisms, plus books on church history, ethics, philosophy, spirituality, and critical essays. They even published an array of Catholic poetry and fiction.

Frank and Masie saw an opportunity to release an untold amount of spiritual growth among English-speaking Christians in writing for educated people. And they accepted the challenge.

Whatever we do in our lifetimes to improve our world is an expression of our love of God. "Our ethical life is a productive activity," says Edward Vacek. "Since God has been involved in evolution, our love for God requires cooperation with God's activity in building up the world."[41]

Lovers want to do something for the ones they love, and that includes the God we love. If we love God, we also want God to be enhanced. In the tradition view, such enhancement was said to be impossible, since God was considered incapable of enrichment. After all, they said, God was already perfect and complete in every way. That tradition insisted that we and our work to move human life forward could make no difference to God, only to our children.

In contrast, Teilhard insists that our worldly successes do make a difference to God. They are important to God and not just to us or to our posterity. The supreme dignity of human work and effort, then, is that it is inherently Christogenic.[42]

But how are we to think about God and the nature of God? What kind of God chooses to create an evolving universe made of matter?

BASIC PRINCIPLE 5:
Love Is the Very Nature of God

Although the church never denied that God was all-loving and all-forgiving, traditional teachers and preachers often chose to focus on God as a strict judge, as one who could assign us to hell as easily as welcome us into heaven. This course of action led to a fear-based spirituality and ethic where God was viewed more as a severe ruler than as an unconditional lover. It created a personal morality almost exclusively focused on sin and forgiveness.

This kind of anxiety-generating spirituality had been dominant in the church since the Middle Ages, and it remained dominant until some years after Teilhard's death in 1955. Only after Vatican II in the 1960s did a shift start to happen. We began to focus on God as loving and merciful, with Jesus as our brother rather than our judge.

Once we acknowledge that the very nature of God is love (see 1 John 2:18—3:20; 4:7—12), a major shift happens. It becomes obvious that God wants our love much more than our anxiety and fear.[43] A loving God enlists our cooperation in the divine project. God invites our personal involvement in that work.[44]

For Teilhard, if God is love, then whatever God creates must be imbued with love. Creation may not yet be perfect, but it is infused with love. The universe must be permeated with God's love energy, and it must be the divine Spirit of love that is driving the divine project.[45]

Teilhard recognized that "love is the most universal, the most tremendous and the most mysterious of the cosmic forces."[46] God is the divine, transcendent source of love that energizes evolution. God's love "draws an entire universe, and not just human history, toward an unfathomable fulfillment yet to be realized."[47] No other quality or energy besides love can account for the evolutionary nature of God's creation or its purpose.

It may be true that we were made of dust and we will return to dust. More importantly, humans are some of the dust and mud that got to stand up, walk around, and make a difference. And what we are, what we do, and what we accomplish during our lifetime makes a difference to God and what God is doing in the world. In other words, your morality is tied to fulfilling your life's purpose on Earth.

For Teilhard, God, who is infinite Love, "penetrates everything."[48] This implies that the divine Lover is also changed by the activities of people, since every lover is affected by the responses of those he or she loves.

Teilhard is in effect saying that the traditional doctrine of the immutability of God is no longer an appropriate way to characterize God. If God's nature is love, then God must be affected—changed—by the behavior and response of those whom God loves.

Following the theology of John the Evangelist and St. Paul, Teilhard grounds his thinking on a definition of *God as Love*.

In the Gospel according to John, Jesus reaffirms the centrality of love in his theology. Early on in his public ministry, during a secret nighttime visit with Nicodemus (see John 3), Jesus tells Nicodemus that God loves the world and all of creation as much as God loves his divine Son. An astounding assertion! He invites Nicodemus to be "reborn" in this loving Spirit to enter this new ethical mentality. It requires loving one's fellow humans and all of creation the way that God loves them.

Repeatedly, Jesus reminds his disciples of the mutual love continually flowing between him and his heavenly Father, and of the divine loving Spirit that he and the Father share and that unites them (see John 14:15–21). During his final supper with his disciples, he leaves them with only one commandment, a love commandment: "Just as I have loved you, you also should love one another" (John 13:34).

In the letters of John to the Christian communities, the theme of "God is love" occurs again and again. "God is love, and those who abide in love abide in God, and God abides in them" (1 John 4:16).

When Jesus tells us to "abide in love"—*abide* means to "dwell" or "make a permanent home" in love—notice that he is calling us to go beyond the Golden Rule. While the Golden Rule is primarily about behavior, "abide" is all about "union" or Connection. Thus, love involves both action and union. Jesus is saying that action for God's project flows from dwelling in love.

Teilhard might express it by saying that simply doing good works is indeed good, but when good works are done "abiding in love," they become evolutionary. They are evolutionary for two reasons. First, once you start "dwelling" in love, that is, moving in and making a permanent home in love, you cannot help but evolve personally. Second, once you abide in love, you can be sure that your good works are in line with what God wants.

In his letter to the people of Corinth, St. Paul offers a paean to love. While the virtues of faith and hope are very important, says Paul, they are nothing compared to love. Love is the greatest virtue. (The English *virtue* comes from the Latin *virtus*, which means "force, or source of energy.") Thus, love is not merely a quality, but a source of energy—an ability. Moreover, love is eternal. It will be the primary energy shown by everyone in heaven with God (see 1 Cor 13:1–13). Love is what makes heaven *heavenly*.

Although Teilhard does not fully explore some of the basic implications of a "God who is love" in any one place in his writings, it is enough to read Teilhard's *The Divine Milieu* and other essays to begin to grasp the depth of Teilhard's love theology. All you need to do is observe a person who is truly loving and note the variety of its expressions that emerge.[49] By analogy, these qualities of love apply to God as well.

Teilhard suggests that the best way to look at the long-range potential of love is to consider love as a *source of energy*.[50] Physicists define *energy* as "the ability to do work." Just as physical energy is the ability to do physical work, and chemical energy is the ability to do chemical work, so love energy is the ability to do loving work. As St. Ignatius Loyola noted in his *Spiritual Exercises*, "Love is manifested more by deeds than by words."[51] Like Ignatius, Teilhard's spirituality, as does his ethics, calls essentially for a life of action. However, it is action that flows from abiding in love.

As Ignatius put it, Jesuits like Teilhard are called to be "contemplatives in action." To keep Teilhard's insight in mind, instead of referring simply to *love*, we use the term *love energy* for more accuracy, since the energy to act is released by love.

Qualities of Love Energy

Some universal qualities of love energy are obvious—in humans as well as in God. We recognize these qualities in ourselves. If God is pure love energy, then these qualities must also characterize God. As you review these qualities, you can see how they shape an image of God that is very different from the traditional image.

Love energy is attractive. We like to be in the presence of truly loving people and enjoy their welcoming energy. God wants us all to have that attractive energy, for this is the way that others come to know and love God, who is the greatest attractor of all.

Love energy makes connections. Love is always seeking to be connected, to create friendships and other forms of loving relationships. Love is all about forming bonds of union. It is often expressed in smiles, hugs, embraces, and kisses.

Love energy grows more mature and unconditional. It becomes more all-embracing. We should set no limit to the number of loving connections we can make with others. What God wants is for us to be lovingly connected to God and to each other. Showing love to others ranks above pious gestures like rituals, fasting, and sacrifice—even obedience to human-made rules.

One day, Martin de Porres, a Dominican lay brother dedicated to helping the poor, found a poor Indian on the street. He was bleeding to death from a dagger wound. Martin took him to his own room in the Dominican priory until he could transport him to his sister's hospice. The prior, when he heard of this, reprimanded Martin for disobedience to priory rules. Martin replied, "Forgive my error, and please instruct me, for I did not know that the precept of obedience took precedence over that of love." Humbled by this reply, the prior gave Martin liberty from then on to follow his inspirations in his works of mercy and love.

Love energy accepts love from another at whatever the level of maturity of that person. In the last chapter of John's Gospel, there is a wonderful story about a dialogue between the risen Lord and Peter. The risen Lord reflects the love energy of God. The story's true poignancy is captured only in the Greek text.[52] In the first exchange, Jesus asks Peter, "Do you love me with unconditional love [*agape* love]?" and Peter, who had betrayed Jesus in the courtyard at his trial and could not claim to love him unconditionally, answers in all honesty, "I love you as a brother [with *philia* love]." A second time, Jesus asks Peter, "Do you love me with unconditional love [*agape* love]?" and Peter answers again in all honesty, "You know I love you as a brother [with *philia* love]." But the third exchange is different. Jesus asks Peter, "Do you love me as a brother [with *philia* love]?" Now, a relieved Peter can acknowledge his brotherly love in all honesty. And he says an unequivocal yes. The point is that Jesus—and God—is willing to accept love at whatever level we offer it. Jesus also assures Peter that Peter will grow into unconditional love (*agape* love) and eventually give his life as an expression of that love.

Love energy is self-expressive. Love energy cannot contain itself but must manifest itself in words and behavior. The most fundamental message in Hebrew Scripture in the first chapter of the Book of Genesis is that God is self-expressive. God creates humans in God's own image and likeness. This creative act of God—making us like God—is a self-expression of God. Sharing God's own image and likeness has little to do with physical appearance, since God is pure spirit. Rather, it refers to God self-sharing with humans *the essential self-expressive love energy that is of the very nature of God.* We are hardwired to love and to express that love outwardly.

Love energy is creative. Love wants to bring new things into the world. It wants to express itself outside itself. That is what God's love did in creating an evolving universe. Creating is what we humans do all our lives. Love is why married couples want to have children. Love is the main reason why people invent things, to express outside themselves what is inside. The same is true of artists and musicians. The same is true of people who write books or do scientific research or prepare a special dinner for a family gathering. They want to create something tangible that gives evidence of their love. With the discovery that God created an evolving universe comes the insight that humans, made in the loving image and likeness of God, are meant to be a creative force in that evolutionary process.

Love energy urges us on to more—more growth, more being, a fuller life, and a deeper consciousness.[53] Love does not stop using the law of Attraction-Connection-Complexity-Consciousness after one cycle. Love never grows static. It keeps cycling at higher and higher levels and expressing itself at those new levels. Love is not satisfied with the status quo. Love energy is an evolutionary force. Teilhard says love is *evolutive*.[54]

Neither is God satisfied with the status quo of the love relationship God has with us. Divine love will keep challenging us to keep growing and expanding in our ability to love until, at the completion of God's project, we will experience what Teilhard called "a paroxysm of love," a divine heart-bursting explosion of love.

Less Obvious Qualities of Love Energy

Other qualities of love energy are perhaps less obvious than the ones listed above but are just as universal.

Love energy complexifies.[55] Each time you make a new friend, you add Complexity to your life. You need to find time to spend with this new friend. Your friend may have interests or values to which you may need to open your mind and heart. Your friend may introduce you to other people who have different ideas, new values, and ways of doing things. All this new experience requires expanding your Consciousness and stretching your understanding.

51

Each of these factors brings more Complexity into your life—and of course into your friend's life as well.

Love energy pushes for growth in consciousness. Once a Connection is made, the Complexity of relationship needs to be understood and integrated into one's mind and heart. In this Consciousness-expanding process, one begins to understand the Attractive power of love energy and the challenge of forming, nurturing, maintaining, and developing loving relationships. One sign of a growth in Consciousness is expressed in the following realization.

Love energy doesn't judge, categorize, or label another person. It accepts and embraces the person *where* they are and *as* they are. Between parents and young children, the more mature love of the parent learns to set boundaries for those less immature ("I'm sorry, but doing your homework is more important than playing video games tonight"), while offering them acceptable alternative behaviors to follow that will challenge them to grow in consciousness.[56]

Love energy is evolutionary. Love of its very nature is open to the future. It wants to evolve, to become richer, deeper, and more welcoming. It is what people mean when they say to another, "I love you more and more each day," or "Over our years together, I have learned to be more compassionate and forgiving." This insight means that the loving person is meant continually to develop and grow in the ability to generate and manifest love at higher levels.

Relationships formed in love must continue to find new ways for the creative self-expression of their love energy, otherwise such a loving relationship may stagnate or grow sick and bitter. This has happened to many marriages that began in mutual love but ended with partners alienated from or even hating one another.

For Teilhard, a primary purpose of ethics is to learn how to form loving relationships as well as how to nurture and deepen them. Teilhard would teach people how to recognize the needs of a relationship and how to provide for those needs.

An individual has at least five levels of needs: (1) physical needs;___ (2) safety and security needs; (3) belongingness needs; (4) self-esteem needs; and (5) self-actualization needs. A relationship also has a similar set of needs on all these five levels in order to grow and make its positive mark on the world.

For example: (1) the couple needs to spend physical time together doing things that emphasize them *as a couple*; (2) partners need to reassure each other that they will work to keep their relationship *safe and secure*; (3) the couple needs to have a family/community to which they *belong*; (4) they each need to *value* their relationship and be part of a community that values their relationship; (5) the couple needs to find ways to develop and *actualize* themselves as a couple by making a contribution *as a couple* to their families and to the community.[57]

In summary, Teilhard tells us that divine love is the energy that first created the world. And it will be divine love cooperating with and inspiring human love that will transform the world.

BASIC PRINCIPLE 6:
The Universe Is a Love Project

The basic principle 6 is a logical step from principle 5. For, if love is the very nature of God, then anything God created would have to be an act of love. Nevertheless, it is important to develop this basic principle in and for itself, especially because God's project is still in process. And that process raises questions. Some with moral implications.

For example, how can an evolutionary project with all its inherent randomness, diminishments, and death be an expression of divine love? Isn't that the question people of faith always ask: "If God really loves us, why does God let bad things happen to us?"

From a traditional perspective, if God has a project at work on ___ Earth, it would be to get as many people "saved" as possible, and to be rid of all the others who fail the test for heaven. The traditional system is very simple: *salvation is all about individual souls.* Each soul must qualify for heaven and life with God or be assigned a failing grade and get rejected. In this traditional approach to spirituality, we're all working for ourselves: "Save your own soul." "Take care of number one."

"Too bad if others don't make the grade." Notice how this produces a very subjective and self-focused way of living.

If God is love, however, then the purpose and goal of God's project is the active loving union of all creation. It is a relational project. *It is all about building loving relationships.* An all-loving God's aim must be continual growth in everyone's ability to love, to become ever more all-embracing of others. Yes, God already loves every individual, but the aim of the divine project is to *get people loving each other.* It involves individuals working together with loving purpose to transform the world in love. Only loving teamwork can bring all creatures and creation together in one great loving union.

Thomas Merton says that if someone wants to know what is meant by "God's will," here is his simple answer: "God's will is certainly found in anything that is required of us in order that we may be united with one another in love."[58]

Teilhard realized that his evolutionary law of Attraction-Connection-Complexity-Consciousness is in fact a law of love, because those same four stages explain the way love operates. Love essentially begins with Attraction and leads to Connection. "The first essential is that the human units involved in the process shall draw closer together, not merely under the pressure of *external* forces, or solely by the performance of material acts, but directly, center to center, through *internal* attraction."[59]

Ilia Delio underlines this observation: "Teilhard realized that if there were no internal propensity to unite, even at a rudimentary level—indeed in the molecule itself—it would be physically impossible for love to appear higher up, in a hominized form."[60]

Teilhard describes these "forces of attraction between [humans to be] as powerful in their own way as nuclear energy appears to be."[61]

In contrast to the traditional subjective and self-focused spirituality, Teilhard proposes an interpersonal and group-focused spirituality, which demands a new way of looking at morality and ethics.

Jesus said, "By this everyone will know that you are my disciples, if you have love for one another" (John 13:35). Jesus calls this "a new commandment." At first glance, the "new commandment" as stated sounds like the Golden Rule. But it is much more. What's new in this commandment is that Jesus is asking his disciples to "love one another...*as I have loved you*" (v. 34, emphasis added). Natural law focuses on basic fairness or *brotherly love* (*philia*), while Jesus's love calls for a generosity of response from his disciples that goes far beyond the basic requirements of the Golden Rule. Jesus's call is to *unconditional love* (*agape*). Some examples of these generously loving (*agape*) responses are mentioned in the Sermon on the Mount—selfless service, going the extra mile, giving more than what is asked for, endless forgiveness of others.

If God could not be intimately related to what is going on in creation and the accomplishment of God's project, God would be less than the fullness of being. For Teilhard, our lives and our work, therefore, fill out God's relational self.[62] Perhaps a metaphor may help explain this divine relationship with the divine project.

God did not create a universe as if it were a wind-up toy that God assembled, cranked up, put on the floor, let it do its thing, then walked away uninterested. As you know, a wind-up toy's actions are essentially fixed and predictable, and watching it soon becomes boring. We know that such toys eventually become boring even to the youngest children. We can be sure that a brilliant God would be bored with such a predictable universe. Thanks to science, we know that God did not create a wind-up universe whose actions are essentially fixed and predictable.

God created a universe that is continually evolving and endlessly fascinating—even to God. It is a universe in which God is intimately interested and involved. God wants the universe to achieve its ultimate purpose and evolve into a creation that is driven by love and filled with love.

God is personally invested in its success. Just as financial investors put money into start-up companies, God continues to pump love into the universe. Just as financial investors do not actually run a company's day-to-day operations, God does not micromanage the universe or human lives. Just as financial investors, who are personally involved in the company's success, put their faith and trust in the people running the company, so God, who is personally involved in the project's success, puts divine faith and trust in the human family. God relates to us less like a toy maker and more like an investor.

It is important to notice a paradox in loving that applies to God as well as to humans. Achieving the fullness of being in union with others requires a suffering or emptying of self. In the incarnation, the Word of God, who is fullness of life, emptied himself in becoming a limited human being. The paradox is that the divine Son emptied himself to show us the Father's fullness of love.

In Jesus, God also shows how it is necessary for us to empty ourselves of our own "fullness" to truly love others. This emptying of self may often require some form of suffering—or even "dying"—to manifest one's love for others. This begins to explain the meaning of Jesus's paradoxical statement: "For those who want to save their life will lose it, and those who lose their life for my sake will find it" (Matt 16:25). The one who refuses to empty oneself of self-concern and self-preservation, when asked to truly love another, has already "lost his [true source of] life."

Fortunately, there are many who are willing to empty themselves of their self-importance and entitlement to love others and creation. In their helping to build the Body of Christ they will find the fullness of life.

This is the paradox of the kingdom of God: self-emptying and abundance of life go together. This paradox is manifest in the incarnation, suffering, death, and resurrection of Jesus: *the abundance of life is found through self-emptying* (the Greek word for *self-emptying* is *kenosis*)—sometimes to the point of suffering and death.

A parable, using an event familiar to any farmer or gardener, describes the same combining of *kenosis* and abundance, As Jesus points out, "Unless a grain of wheat falls into the earth and dies, it remains just a single grain; but if it dies, it bears much fruit" (John 12:24). Abundance comes through self-emptying.

One of the most challenging acts of kenosis required of persons living a truly evolutionary life is *letting go of the desire to remain a separate autonomous individual*. Much self-emptying will be required if we humans are to become as all-embracing as our heavenly Creator. God passionately loves all humans, all animals, all plants, and all beings in the cosmos. One's level of moral and ethical growth is measured by how all-embracing one's love is. It is this kind of love toward which we are being called, namely, to welcome more and more people into our hearts, even those we do not like. We are to come to love the world and its development passionately.[63]

Teilhard says that we learn to love humanity and the world by fostering its development. This is a process that he calls *cosmogenesis*, that is, helping creation to reach its maturity. But Teilhard's theological insight is that in our work and suffering, we contribute to the development of the Body of Christ, which he calls *Christogenesis*.[64]

Once we accept the fact of evolution operating at every level of being in our world, our ethical focus shifts from a primacy on saving our souls by avoiding sin, to a primacy on cooperating with what God is doing on Earth, namely, building the Earth into a loving unity of all people. We are shifting from a focus on *self* (saving one's soul) to a focus on *cooperating with others* (in helping foster what God is doing in the world).

Since the divine project continues to evolve, expressions of divine love must be evolving as God continues to relate to humanity in the shared pursuit of the project's goal. In other words, divine love changes its way of relating to the Body of Christ as the Body matures and complexifies, just as parents change their way of relating to their children as their children mature and their lives become more involved with others. Growth in union among the human members of Christ's Body is the unity that God desires.

God's project is a love project. Our moral challenge is to grow in love so that our love becomes as "perfect"—or as all-embracing—as that of our heavenly Father.

In the English translations from the Latin and Greek, Jesus encourages us to "be perfect, therefore, as your heavenly Father is perfect" (Matt 5:48). The original Aramaic word Jesus used for "perfect" has a few possible meanings. Two other possible translations would be "all-embracing" or "all-encompassing," either of which translations would fit more appropriately as Jesus's summation of his sermon in Matthew 5—7. As humans, we can never aspire to be as perfect as the Father, but we can at least continue to grow and evolve in becoming ever more "all-embracing" or "all-encompassing" in our ability to love.

BASIC PRINCIPLE 7:
A Planetary Mind and Heart
(The Noosphere)

A planetary mind and heart (the noosphere) has arisen and is evolving.

Jesus proposed a radically new way of living the moral life. For Teilhard, Jesus's "way" is ideal for an evolutionary world created by Love and for loving. His heavenly Father created the universe for a purpose.

The Father had a plan for creation. Creation is, in fact, a divine project and that project is in process. It has been evolving since the beginning of time. Jesus knows the Father's intent. And Jesus reveals to us the Father's wish that the divine project become manifest—be revealed. Jesus referred to this divine project as "the kingdom of God" or "the kingdom of heaven." For Teilhard, *at present the divine project happens to be focused on evolving the mind and heart of humanity.*

Noosphere is a term coined by Teilhard to describe the evolving *mind and heart of the planet.*[65] He saw the noosphere as a layer—like the atmosphere—that completely covers Earth. The noosphere layer is different from the more familiar layers of land, water, atmosphere, and biological life. The noosphere envelopes our world is an evolving *thinking and feeling layer,* an incredibly complex palpable field of thought and emotions shaping a newly emerging global consciousness. The appearance of this new global consciousness was predicted by Teilhard early in the twentieth century. For him, it is as though humanity is beginning to develop a single planetary mind and heart.

The power and universal presence of a global mind has become more evident each year. Today's many forms of social media are facilitating a milieu of communication and connection that is evolving very quickly. The global mind is symbolized by the hundreds of communication satellites that daily orbit our planet, connecting everyone in the world into one great, ever-expanding, and unbelievably interwoven network of thought and emotion. That's the noosphere growing, developing, and maturing.[66] In Teilhard's own words, "With every day that passes it becomes a little more impossible for us to act or think otherwise than collectively."[67]

Until now, traditional morality and ethics have been concerned with an individual's choices and actions, and their direct effects on individuals in the family and local community. Without denying this fact, Teilhard pointed out that the evolving noosphere has enabled us—one might even say forced us—daily to become conscious of the concerns and needs of just about everyone on Earth. The noosphere requires a morality and ethics that involves the entire humanity.

Because of the noosphere, we are no longer familiar only with the thoughts, feelings, and concerns of the people around us. We also are aware of the concerns and interest of the hundreds and thousands of people we encounter on Facebook, Twitter, e-mail, news broadcasts, and other social media. Each day, we are invited inside the minds and hearts of people all over the world. Our actions on social media can affect people anywhere in the world, some we may never meet face-to-face.

Today, not only are individual lives intertwined, but also nations themselves. Nations are interdependent financially because the vitality of each major global financial market influences the health of all the others. Decisions of persons who get elected in one nation can influence other nations far away. Medically, because of constant international travel, a contagious disease that starts in one small area of the world may be carried quickly to every continent and become a planetary epidemic. At the same time, research to find a pharmaceutical intervention to stop such a disease may be carried out simultaneously and cooperatively in many laboratories around the globe. Spiritually, people of many different religions are sprinkled throughout each country. Hopefully, instead of fearing and mistrusting each other, people are gradually learning to respect and learn from each other.

If emotions run high in some part of the world, we all get to hear and watch—and we wonder how it might affect us. If there is a famine or medical epidemic happening on the other side of the globe, we are aware of it and respond generously, as if those suffering were our neighbors. This is the noosphere in action.

As a species, we are moving from a national mentality ("America is the most powerful nation in the world") to a global mentality ("We need to care for the health of our planet"). We no longer see ourselves merely as separate nations but as one world, one people, one immense complex—and conscious—family. This is manifest in world organizations such as the General Assembly of the United Nations and the International Criminal Court in The Hague. Noospheric thinking is found in manufacturing in the formation of world trade agreements, in global issues such as hundreds of nations meeting out of concern for the planet's climate, ecology, environment, and pollution. Certain nations are making commitments that benefit the planet, sometimes at the price of their own nations.

Over thirty years ago, in 1982, Peter Russell announced this shift from a national mindset to a planetary mindset in his book *The Global Brain Awakens*.[68] Teilhard might express it differently, perhaps by saying that the noosphere has gradually become consciously aware of itself. Humanity itself has begun to think and feel and act as one mind and heart.

Morality and ethics are no longer individual or local concerns. We are concerned for humanity. Humanity is trying to develop a planetary Self, a global sense of identity, a world Ego. We are probably just in the infantile stage in this process, but it continues to grow.[69]

We cannot stop the noosphere from evolving, for we as the human family are inevitably becoming more and more intricately interwoven with each other.[70] "The Noosphere can function only by releasing more and more spiritual energy with an ever-higher potential."[71]

Teilhard doesn't discuss sin in this context, but I suspect that he would say that sin and other forms of diminishment will remain active among us until the very last moments in the completion of God's project. Teilhard would prefer to envision a progressive lessening of sin. In his view, as humanity becomes more united in love and abiding in love, the prevalence of sin will likely decrease. His point is that, despite every evolutionary delay and detour imaginable, God continues to call the people living in every age to love one another and creation more and more unconditionally. For Teilhard, the success of God's project is inevitable. God will never give up investing in the divine project. However, in its unfolding, the process may have to endure many unexpected twists and turns and will require human cooperation up to the very last moment.

Thus, for Teilhard, because of the noosphere, the shape of moral and ethical life will become more global and forward-looking. Morality and ethics from now on will be all about connection, union, unity, oneness. The movement is toward humanity growing into one mind and one heart. For Teilhard, we are slowly growing into the mind and heart of the Cosmic Christ.

Traditionally, we applied the word *salvation* to individuals. In its root meaning, *salvation* means "attaining the fullness of life, or wholeness." However, Teilhard sees salvation as primarily a collective process. We grow into the fullness of life only in relationship. On a grander scale, salvation means individuals and groups freely participating in *cosmogenesis* and *Christogenesis*. These two processes generate a collective stream of life that is ascending toward its completion or, more precisely, its *fullness* or *wholeness*.

Wholeness is really a term meant to describe relationships, not individuals. Here, it describes a process of humanity being incorporated into God's evolving world. As Teilhard writes, "We are spiritualized by being carried along by the spiritualization of all things. We are united to Christ by entering communion with all people. We will be saved by an option that has chosen that total communion."[72]

BASIC PRINCIPLE 8:
Unire as a Foundation of Metaphysics

In an evolutionary world, *unire* provides a better foundation of metaphysics, theology, and ethics than *esse*.

A Metaphysics Based on Love

Teilhard developed a spirituality and an ethic founded on a God whose nature is love—or loving energy. He realized that for many centuries traditional Christian metaphysics was based on the approach of Thomas Aquinas and the Thomists. They saw God as the perfection of *Being* (in Latin, *Esse*). One's definition of God becomes the basis of one's metaphysics, theology, spirituality, and ethics. In the Thomistic view, which eventually became the church's view, God had to be defined as the perfection of Oneness, Truth, Goodness, and Beauty. In Thomistic philosophical tradition, these four are the most important qualities of a perfectly transcendent Being (*Esse*). God is therefore described as all-powerful, all-knowing, all-seeing, all-wise, all-present, and so on. In this tradition, God is often defined by negation, by the fact that God is *un*-limited, *un*-attainable, *un*-comprehendible, and so on.

Teilhard recognized the inadequacies of this abstract and transcendent approach to the nature of God when dealing with an evolving world. He recognized the need to break radically from this tradition of a God defined by perfection and negation. He offers a definition of God as Unconditional Love, thereby providing an alternative basis for metaphysics. For Teilhard, *unire* (Latin for "to unite or join"), provides a more adequate metaphysical basis to describe a God whose nature is *love energy*.

In Teilhard's words, "What comes first in the world for our thought is not 'being' but 'the union which produces this being.' Let us, therefore, try to replace a metaphysics of *Esse* with a metaphysics of *Unire* (to unite or connect) or *Uniri* (to be united)."[73] However, Teilhard never really fully developed this novel approach to metaphysics. Its fuller development is essential, but the detailed work remains to be done. Teilhard leaves doing this detailed work as a challenge to us who live today.

For Thomists and a God of perfect Being (*Esse*), the prominent virtues for people to practice are prudence, temperance, fortitude, and wisdom. For Teilhard and the New Testament writers, in contrast, the prominent virtues for a believer include the many forms of loving union, such as mercy, compassion, forgiveness, and healing.[74] How are we to account for this change in the hierarchy of virtues?

The discovery that God did not create a "perfect" universe but an evolving one—and one in need of healing—also challenged Teilhard to clarify a new understanding of the divine nature. Teilhard realized this challenge. He saw how inadequate a theology starting from God as perfect Being (*Esse*) is to an evolving creation.

He also realized that starting with a God who is perfect Being makes it difficult to grasp the nature of the God of the Scriptures, a God whose essential nature is love. What is most important to God in the Hebrew Scriptures is God's relationship with God's people and their fidelity to that relationship. Loving energy is all about forming loving relationships. The Holy Trinity is itself a relationship continually uniting (*unire*) in love—within its divine Self as well as with humanity and all of creation.

In classical and traditional metaphysics, God is a perfect Being. In this image of God as perfect Being, God is seen as totally transcendent from the rest of the finite created world. God is above it all. God and creation are quite separate. After a person dies, God is the judge who decides where the soul shall spend eternity—either in heaven adoring God forever or in a painful eternal hell. In this traditional approach, God is not concerned with creation but only with the fate of each human soul.

In an evolving universe, God who is Love is constantly involved with creation and its various beings and species and their relationships that continue to emerge in the evolutionary process. In God's project, the fullest maturity of creation will be expressed as a loving union of all creatures. These creatures will have love for each other and for God. Thus, for Teilhard, a far more appropriate moral basis for the Judeo-Christian tradition is not "being" but "loving union."

In this new metaphysics, the basis of spirituality and the moral life is love of God and love of each other. "Love the Lord your God with all your heart, and with all your soul, and with all your strength, and with all your mind; and your neighbor as yourself" (Luke 10:27).[75] Notice that God is not asking for obedience, sacrifice, worship, adoration, or anything else, but only for love. And God wants total love. In turn, God wants us to learn to express love to everyone and everything. God is calling us to grow toward an all-embracing love. Thus, the need to shift to a metaphysics of union (*unire*).

Nevertheless, there is a great desire deep within us to have "more being" (more *esse*). And Teilhard is aware of that desire. We want to experience life and existence more fully, more deeply. However, as Teilhard points out, this deepening (more being) happens only in relationships. Our being is best enriched as we mature into higher levels of love that can only happen in relationships (unions). It can happen only on levels of love that become more all-embracing of people, animals, and all of creation. In a letter to a friend, Teilhard wrote that it was becoming more necessary in our spirituality "to know Earth like we know our own body."[76]

In this regard, Teilhard said that believers today who had a "zest for life"[77] would look for a religion "which activates them most as human beings." These are the people who, through "their eagerness to live," contribute "something irreplaceable to God."[78] For Teilhard, the way we come to experience "more being" (more *esse*) and a zest for life is through "more union" (more *unire*) because more being comes through more union. That is the way love works. We experience more being the more all-embracing our love grows.

Love, even its most immature expressions—childhood playmates, social acquaintances, physical attraction, fan clubs, Facebook friends—requires joining, participating, and connecting. These are the pathways to closeness, oneness, union. In fact, to bring people together in loving connection (*unire*) becomes the central activity of God's project as well as the primary activity of God.[79]

Although love because of union brings about "more being" (*esse*), it is much more important to the divine project that love brings about "more union" (*unire*). In other words, it is important that social acquaintances grow into friendships, that physical attraction grows into emotional closeness, and that Facebook friends come together to work in larger social projects.

For Teilhard, evolutionary success of God's project is defined in terms of growth in union among humans. Scientific inventions and technological advancements are almost always intended to help bring people together in enjoyable, peaceful, and productive unions. Mark Zuckerberg invented Facebook, first, so that fellow students at Harvard would have a convenient way to stay connected to each other. Eventually, Facebook expanded so that people anywhere in the world could stay connected.

Some technologies like air conditioning, water purifiers, and healthy food production methods are designed to improve the quality of life. Other technologies like healthful drugs and vaccines provide compassion and care. Others like television and internet search engines produce growth in knowledge, and so on. All of these are useful, even essential, to God's project.

The most important part of moral living becomes discovering new ways to love and support one another in various forms of union or connection. This will inevitably require us to make sacrifices in our lives to build the future. Our nature pushes us to discover new unities and to be open to ever further evolution.

The criterion Teilhard uses to identify a development as positive is whether the new "union," brought about by love, releases "more being." This desire to create more being through more union is, essentially, what Teilhard means by the "love of evolution" or living "evolutely."[80]

Once Teilhard established that "forming loving unions" (*Unire*) as the basis of ethics, he was able to reconcile Christian theology with God creating an evolving universe. If *Esse* is assumed to be the basic nature of God, there is little need for God to create any universe at all, since God is totally complete in God's self!

A Love-filled Creation

With a metaphysical foundation of *Unire*, people can more easily grasp the reasons why God, a pure loving spirit, would create an evolving material universe. What modern science tells us is that the physical matter of creation—every subatomic particle—must be imbued with *Unire*, the divine loving spirit, because everything in creation is driven to create unions.[81]

The earliest unions, according to science, would be primarily physical ones, such as subatomic particles uniting to form atoms. But the connecting process doesn't stop there. Atoms unite to form molecules,

molecules interact to form compounds, and so on. These unions would eventually unite symbiotically into life forms. Over many eons of time, such living unions would develop movement and sensations, including touch, taste, smell, hearing, and vision. Eventually, these multiple sensory inputs would unite to form perceptions, and multiple perceptions would unite to form concepts. Conceptual thought and imagination would eventually evolve and emerge for the first time in humans as self-reflective consciousness.

The divine love energy operated through billions of years to keep evolution moving toward its divine purpose. In creation, God was not simply creating elements that had "being" (*esse*) but elements seeking "union" (*unire*). These unions would, in turn, unite to create evermore complex and conscious unions. Eventually, Teilhard believed, there would come a moment in future time when humans would realize that they had become one collective human consciousness. One grand union.[82]

In Teilhard's own inimitable style, "Mankind [forms] a single, major organic unity, enclosed upon itself; a single, hyper-complex, hyper-centered, hyper-conscious arch-molecule, co-extensive with the heavenly body [Earth] on which it was born."[83] For Teilhard, developing that one collective human planetary consciousness—and conscience—is the major objective for humans at this period in our history.[84]

With these eight basic Teilhardian principles supporting our thinking, we are ready to explore the basic principles of Teilhard's ethics and moral theology.

4

Eleven Principles of Teilhard's Ethics

A S YOU CAN see from Teilhard's eight basic principles, his thinking is focused less on a *theology of individual salvation* and much more on a *theology to accomplish a divine project*. Morally, Teilhard is less interested in answering the question, "What happens to my soul at death?" and more interested in "How can I contribute to helping accomplish God's project during my lifetime on Earth?" It is more centered on what God wants *from* me than on what I want from God *for* me. It is all about us actively helping bring about the kingdom of God. It is focused on honoring and carrying out our promise to God every time we say in the Lord's Prayer, "Thy will be done on Earth."

For many, the changes Teilhard proposes may require a major shift in moral and ethical thinking. This is especially true for those brought up on and committed to a more traditional moral approach to life. From the traditional standpoint, "Thy will be done" primarily means avoiding sin. In an evolutionary ethic, "Thy will be done" requires putting on a new mind, a higher mind, a *meta* (higher) *noia* (mindset).[1] Teilhard offers some guiding principles to help develop this "God's project" mindset.

The following eleven moral and ethical principles, derived from Teilhard's writings, provide a basic guide for persons making moral decisions and actions during their lifetime. Each principle is discussed in detail after a few preparatory sections.

Teilhard's Ethical Principles

ETHICAL PRINCIPLE 1: Ethics is about guiding human choices and behavior to make a positive difference in helping promote and advance God's evolutionary project.

ETHICAL PRINCIPLE 2: An evolutionary ethics is focused on each person taking positive action to make a positive difference, alone and with others.

ETHICAL PRINCIPLE 3: The moral call is to be willing to try anything that offers hope for advancing God's project.

ETHICAL PRINCIPLE 4: Two primary ethical responsibilities shared by every person are (1) to build and maintain an ever-expanding loving human community; and (2) to care for the health and welfare of the planet (to love matter).

ETHICAL PRINCIPLE 5: In addition, each one, according to his or her resources of love energy, is morally obliged to nurture the evolutionary process.

ETHICAL PRINCIPLE 6: Everyone has many resources for nurturing the evolutionary process.

ETHICAL PRINCIPLE 7: One's ethical obligations may change over time, depending on one's change in available resources or level of spiritual growth.

ETHICAL PRINCIPLE 8: In an evolutionary ethic, the primary personal sins are sins of omission.

ETHICAL PRINCIPLE 9: Confronting social sin is especially important in an evolutionary world.

ETHICAL PRINCIPLE 10: People operate morally at various levels of spiritual maturity and consciousness.

ETHICAL PRINCIPLE 11: A major purpose for acts of healing, forgiveness, mercy—toward the sick, grieving, rejected, orphans, widows, the unemployed, and so on—is to enable recipients of our care to rejoin the community so that they may make their unique loving contribution to God's project.

Six Observations

1. *Teilhard's ethical principles apply to all human beings, no matter what their religion or lack of it.*[2] God has a plan or project to be carried out on Earth, and God invites all human beings to cooperate in this work.[3] God has planted within every person the drive to make a positive difference in the world.[4] It follows that every human being has an active role to play in this work. God is not calling only religious people to help renew the face of Earth, but everyone, even nonbelievers and atheists. God has implanted the desire to do good into every human mind and heart.

For example, some atheist writers who have made a positive difference in the world include Isaac Azimov, James Baldwin, Simone de Beauvoir, Albert Camus, Anton Chekov, Arthur Clarke, Joseph Conrad, Daniel Dennett, Christopher Hitchens, Heinrik Ibsen, Jack London, Arthur Miller, Philip Roth, Maurice Sendak, Salman Rushdie, Robert Louis Stevenson, Tom Wolfe, and Virginia Woolf.

Scores of famous men and women in science and technology—biologists, physicists, anthropologists, astronomers, chemists, physicians, mathematicians—have publicly identified themselves as atheists, and their atheism may even be relevant to their notable activities or contributions to public life. Many are Nobel Prize winners or recipients of other humanitarian and scientific awards. Yet they all claim to be atheists. Among them are the following: quantum physicist Niels Bohr; biologist Francis Crick, who codiscovered the structure of the DNA molecule; psychologist Albert Ellis; quantum mechanics scientist Richard Feynman; psychoanalyst Sigmund Freud; psychologist Erich Fromm; mathematician and physicist Stephen Hawking; physicist Peter Higgs, who is known for his prediction of the existence of a new particle, the Higgs boson, ironically nicknamed the "God particle"; chemist Linus Pauling, recipient of the Nobel Peace Prize; mathematical physicist Roger Penrose, whose formulas facilitate many astronomical calculations; analytic philosopher Bertrand Russell; neurologist and famous author Oliver Sacks; computer inventor Alan Turing; biologist Craig Venter, one of the first researchers to sequence the human genome; and chemist James Watson, codiscoverer of the DNA.

You do not need to know consciously that you are helping to move God's project toward its fulfillment, only that you carry out your purpose in life. God's invitation to contribute is written in each person's heart, as well as in their genes, their experiences, and their culture.

2. *In Teilhard's ethical principles, there are no lists of personal sins, named or even suggested, as one might find in a traditional moral theology textbook used in seminaries.* Teilhard is not denying that it is a breach of the moral law and a rejection of God's love to violate another's trust or reputation by lying, cheating, murdering, committing adultery, being physically and sexually abusive, and the rest. Teilhard's point is that God's focus is not on our failures, our weaknesses, or our sins, but on the accomplishment of God's evolutionary project.

During any day, one's moral and ethical decisions and actions may be large or small. They may involve simple interactive behaviors of caring and compassion as well as major decisions. Each action, large or small, intending to make a positive difference in the world contributes to God's project if it is done with good will. For Teilhard, God's primary interest centers on the moral obligation inherent in each one's capacity to foster that divine project personally and in cooperation with others.

Suppose, for example, God's project was to build a house and you were a roofing expert. Teilhard's moral principles are focused on you using your talents to help build the roof of God's house. Getting God's house built should be your most important moral concern. You may have weaknesses and failures in certain areas of your life. So does everyone else. We are all frail and finite creatures, and we strive to improve ourselves. But according to Teilhard's ethical principle, doing your "roofing work" is your primary moral and ethical responsibility as part of the construction team.[5]

3. *Although prayer is essential in one's spiritual practices, the core of moral living in an evolutionary world consists in one's actions and choices.* During prayer, one chooses to make a positive difference in one's life, the community, and the planet. God's project involves transforming the world in love.[6] For Teilhard, our job as moral persons is to join in this grand work together, and to do it for love of God and God's creation. Standing by and watching others do the work is not an acceptable alternative.[7] For many, taking a proactive role is a totally new way of looking at their moral and ethical lives.

God is most forgiving of human weakness and failure, even though many humans and civil laws are not. For instance, you may commit homicide and receive God's forgiveness, but civil law still requires that you serve prison time, if convicted. Humans may have the best of intentions to live to their highest ideals, but as a species we are still inherently weak and morally immature. There is still much cruelty and violence. There are still criminals among us consciously doing evil.

4. God is working with a morally underdeveloped humanity. Teilhard wants us to grow morally, to begin thinking and acting more like God, who treats us with divine mercy. He wants us to begin believing that even humans who have "sinned" want to do good in the world. I suspect that Jesus saw many sinners, including some of his own chosen twelve apostles, not as inherently evil but rather as either weak, emotionally immature, or morally underdeveloped (unripe). Most of us are still morally underdeveloped.[8]

To help such underdeveloped people gain personal self-discipline, develop emotionally, and grow in moral consciousness remains a continually important work for God's project. If that is the kind of work you do, for example, in parenting, teaching, and counseling, you are doing a most important work in God's project. The hope is that, by maturing emotionally and morally, we may contribute more directly and powerfully to the growth of love in the world.

5. These principles apply even to those who are suffering. In 1933, someone asked Teilhard to write an essay on the meaning of suffering. Near the end of his essay, titled "The Meaning and Constructive Value of Suffering," he wrote these astounding words:

> Human suffering, the sum total of suffering poured out at each moment over the whole earth, is like an immeasurable ocean. But what makes up this immensity? Is it blackness, emptiness, barren wastes? No, indeed: it is potential energy. Suffering holds hidden within it, in extreme intensity, the ascensional force of the world.
>
> The whole point is to set this force free by making it conscious of what it signifies and of what it is capable. For if all the sick people in the world were simultaneously to turn their sufferings into a single shared longing for the speedy completion of the kingdom of God through the organizing

of the earth, what a vast leap toward God the world would thereby make![9]

In his insight, Teilhard realized that suffering often requires the expenditure of tremendous amounts of energy. On the cross, Jesus used the energy of his suffering for two purposes: first, for the forgiveness of humanity's sins; and, second, for further energizing God's project in the world.[10] Teilhard realized that humans could similarly direct the energy of their suffering by sharing in Christ's second purpose, namely, by directing their suffering energy, by their intention, toward the success of some part of God's project.[11]

Typically, those who suffer tend to interpret their suffering either as a waste of energy or as a punishment. Teilhard saw in suffering a potential force for good. Teilhard wanted all suffering people to realize how they could use their suffering energy to produce a transformation of the world by their conscious intention. The energy spent in all forms of human suffering, not merely physical pain but also emotional and spiritual pain, may be consciously redirected to the success of God's project.

For Teilhard, while you are breathing, you have work to do for God's project on Earth. Even when you are suffering and physically incapacitated, you can still, consciously and intentionally, direct the energy you spend in your suffering to benefit the work of Christ.[12] You can perform activities of growth.

6. *These ethical principles are meant to serve as guidelines.* Because we live in an evolving universe, these ethical principles of Teilhard's are not fixed rules but general guidelines to help direct daily and long-range decisions and actions. They are not static or fixed. Their meaning and manner of application will change as we evolve, personally and collectively.

Like God, Teilhard is not fixated on your weaknesses and susceptibility to temptations. He is far more concerned about developing your ability to work in helping transform the world in ways that only you can provide.[13]

In the following sections, each ethical principle is discussed and examples of it are given. After each principle is stated, you will find listed those numbers of Teilhard's eight basic principles from which this ethical principle is derived. For your convenience, here again are

71

the eight Teilhard Basic Principles that were more fully developed in chapter 3:

Teilhard's Eight Basic Principles

BASIC PRINCIPLE 1: God created an evolving universe.

BASIC PRINCIPLE 2: The law governing evolution may be summarized as Attraction-Connection-Complexity-Consciousness.

BASIC PRINCIPLE 3: Bringing this evolving universe to its fulfillment is God's project as well as God's purpose for creating the universe.

BASIC PRINCIPLE 4: The task of completing God's evolutionary project requires active human cooperation.

BASIC PRINCIPLE 5: Love is the very nature of God.

BASIC PRINCIPLE 6: The universe is a love project.

BASIC PRINCIPLE 7: A planetary mind and heart (the noosphere) has arisen and is evolving.

BASIC PRINCIPLE 8: In an evolutionary world *unire* provides a better foundation of metaphysics, theology, and ethics than *esse*.

ETHICAL PRINCIPLE 1:
Advancing God's Evolutionary Project

Ethics is about guiding human choices and behavior in such a way that they make a positive difference in helping promote and advance God's evolutionary project. (*Derived from Basic Principles 1, 2, 3, 4, 6*)

In one sense, this first ethical principle summarizes all the others. However, it is important to realize how radically different Teilhard's approach is from traditional moral approaches to life.

Traditionally, the simple rule for moral living was to obey the Ten Commandments and avoid temptations to sin. Its goal was to help you pass the final exam, get into heaven, and, hopefully, leave the world no worse off than you found it. This traditional approach encouraged a sin-focused morality and produced a self-focused spirituality. If getting to heaven was one's most important objective in life, and sin was the one thing that could prevent you from getting there, then one's spiritual life had to be sin-focused. For this reason, it was most important to know which actions were sinful and which were not. And it was just as important to know which sins were mortal and would automatically exclude you from heaven, and which were venial and would put you temporarily in a purgatorial state after death for a period of penitential cleansing before releasing you to heaven.

Following this tradition, chapters in most traditional moral theology textbooks used in seminaries were based on each of the Ten Commandments. Each chapter listed the many possible personal moral violations one could commit in each category as well as their severity. If you were unsure whether a certain action was sinful, it was easy to find the answer. Most church teachings clearly defined an answer to your question.

In this context, the sacrament of confession was crucial because it was the only place where you could get your sins forgiven for a small penance. Only after Vatican II did the church realize that this sacrament proved to be far more valuable when it was used, face-to-face, to foster the spiritual growth of the penitent and not just to get sins erased. It was renamed the sacrament of reconciliation for this reason.

However, once we accept our individual and collective responsibility for moving evolution forward, following Teilhard's first three basic principles, an ethical life requires more than simply staying out of trouble, avoiding sin, and leaving the world no worse than we found it. Checking with your priest, minister, or rabbi to find out if a certain act was sinful or not is no longer enough. Rather, in an evolutionary universe, moral life on Earth is oriented toward improving the world and the quality of life for all living things.

Instead of an ethics of "escape" from the world or "avoidance" of sin, Teilhard proposes an ethics of full "involvement" in the loving transformation of Earth. For him, this transformation is precisely what the Creator, Christ, and the Holy Spirit want from us and are inspiring us to accomplish.[14]

There are, however, morally underdeveloped people who, in their greed for money and power, use their energy and activity simply to become increasingly rich and powerful. They care little either about sin or about enriching the world with love. Their life's purpose is to amass money and possessions.

The following story exemplifies how some people, though brilliant in their own fields, may be quite morally immature and be totally unaware of it.

Some years ago, a friend of ours, a multimillionaire at thirty-five, was convalescing after an illness when he happened to pick up a book on philosophy written by a Russian named Ouspensky.[15] As he was paging through the book he noticed a question that he felt was being proposed to him personally: *What is the purpose of human life, and your life in particular?*

It was a wake-up moment for him. It was the first time he had asked himself the question, *Why am I here on Earth? What am I meant to do with my life?* He wasn't a very religious man, so he was not looking to a church for an answer. He was simply considering the question as a reflective person.

He wondered whether others had been confronted by those powerful questions.

A few weeks later, after he had regained his strength, he was on the golf course with two of his millionaire friends. He casually asked them, "What do you see as your purpose in life? What do you hope to accomplish?"

Without much hesitation, one who owned seventy-five fast food franchises said he hoped to acquire another seventy-five of them. The other companion who owned fifty large apartment buildings in different cities said he hoped to acquire fifty more.

Our friend recognized that his two companions saw no other purpose in their lives than to accumulate more possessions and to become richer and richer. The two men had little concern for their employees or their customers, only that profits kept rolling into their bank accounts.

Realizing, until that moment, that he had been like them in their acquisitive greed, he decided that day that he wanted his life to have more meaning and purpose than merely increasing his wealth. He also realized that he had not yet found a new purpose for his life.

He eventually discovered it, but it took him nearly twenty years before he could clearly identify it. I introduced him to some of Teilhard's ideas and books, and he began to focus his attention on caring for his employees and his customers.

For example, in a restaurant he owned, instead of keeping all the profits for himself, he decided to spread the lion's share of profits with his employees. He kept 15 percent of profits for himself and restaurant improvements. The rest he divided equally among the employees. So the dishwashers and busboys got the same gainshare of profits as the restaurant's manager. Each gainshare was quite small at first, but as employees began to feel that they were, in a sense, being treated as co-owners of the restaurant, the quality of their service improved dramatically. They covered for each other. They helped one another. Fewer dishes were broken. Fewer workers were calling in "sick." Stealing food from the freezer stopped. Fewer employees quit their jobs—in a business where annual employee turnover can be as high as 200 percent. The restaurant grew in popularity, and the amount of gainshare grew month by month. It was said that, after four years, dishwashers were earning almost as much in gainshare as in their paychecks. Incidentally, my friend was making as much profit as ever.

He realized that his employees really ran the restaurant and that they deserved to enjoy the benefits of their efforts. He appreciated them and loved them. He knew most of them by name. Through gainsharing, many employees were able to provide better for their families. Younger employees were able to afford to enroll in nearby colleges. The restaurant became an inspiring place to work. Others who heard about this gainsharing system wanted to work in his restaurant. The waiting list of potential new employees grew longer each week.

The restaurant owner realized that by sharing profits with his employees, he was creating a better life for his employees and setting an example of kindness, compassion, and love. His way of doing business influenced his customers as well, for they kept coming back and bringing their friends. Because of the growing size of his satisfied customers, he never needed to take out an ad in a local newspaper or promote his restaurant on television.

Ethics is about guiding human choices and behavior in such a way that they make a positive difference in helping promote and advance God's evolutionary project.

Spiritual Exercise: A New Life Purpose

Have you ever thought of your life's purpose as helping to transform the world in love? Have you ever thought of your moral and ethical life in

75

*terms of this Teilhardian principle of positive action? If avoidance of
sin had been an earlier focus of your moral life, how would Teilhard's
principle change your attitude?*

ETHICAL PRINCIPLE 2:
Making a Positive Difference

An evolutionary ethics is focused on each person taking positive
action to make a positive difference, alone and with others. *(Derived
from Basic Principles 4, 7)*

———   This principle refocuses your moral and ethical life on what you
can do or could do rather than on what you should not do. For many,
this is a complete reversal of the traditional moral perspective and attitude.

———   Those of us brought up in traditional churches were taught that
if we didn't violate the Ten Commandments or the obligations of our
religious denomination—and we said our prayers—we were morally
upstanding people. Christian ethics was summed up in the phrase,
"Do good and avoid evil." In other words, we were to keep from sin-
ning so that we could go to heaven.

For Teilhard, avoiding sin is only the starting point for living life
in an evolutionary world. His focus centered on the fact that we can
make a positive difference in the growth of love in the world. Teilhard
asks, "Do you want moral rules for conduct?" He replies, "One sentence will serve as an answer: By becoming for God the reinforcement
of evolution."[16] That is the simplest way of describing Teilhard's moral
directive: *Support the evolutionary process.*

Teilhard knows that there will always be temptations to avoid
doing the positive work we could be doing, and we will undoubtedly
succumb to some temptations in our weaker moments. But a God of
love is unconditionally forgiving. Teilhard would argue that when we
are lured away from our true work, we ask God's forgiveness and trust
that God's forgiveness is given. Using a popular expression, Teilhard
might say to us, "If you fail, 'pick yourself up, dust yourself off, and start
all over again.'" In other words, get back to the work you were meant
to be doing for God.

Notice Teilhard's positive, forward-looking approach. He does not encourage self-pity or self-demeaning after a moral failure. His emphasis is on getting back to the work at hand. Rather than simply avoiding negative actions or avoiding temptation to violate the commandments, Teilhard urges us to stay focused on making a positive difference with our lives, to cooperate with the Holy Spirit in "renewing the face of the Earth." Teilhard writes,

> To worship is now becoming to devote oneself body and soul____ to the creative act, associating oneself with that act in order to fulfill the world by hard work and intellectual exploration....To love one's neighbor was formerly to do him no injury and to bind up his wounds. Henceforth charity, without losing any of its compassion, will attain its full meaning in life given for common progress."[17]

Our purpose for living is not to stay out of trouble but rather to become fully involved with human progress in whatever ways we can. "Don't just stand there. Do something." Find a way to improve the situation. If you're stuck, try an alternative way. Make a constructive difference. God has a project for creation. Enlist in the work. Cooperate with God. Say, "Thy will be done on Earth."

For Teilhard, there are two dimensions to your work on Earth: the first involves making and building your own self, and the second involves collaborating in another great work, God's project. Both are to be done at the same time. While the cosmic-sized scope of that divine work infinitely transcends your lifetime of work, nonetheless it is your achievements, along with those of billions of others, that help complete the world.[18]

During the wrenching, divisive, and polarizing months leading up to the United States' elections of 2016, a mistrust and, in some cases, outright hatred of Muslims was peaking across the land. In Georgia, an Indian-born Muslim named Malik Waliyani bought a gas station and convenience store early in the year. A few months later, he arrived one morning to open his business and discovered that his store had been burglarized and damaged. A clear hate crime. Nevertheless, he struggled to keep it open but was having a tough time.

The nearby Baptist congregation, the Smoke Rise Baptist Church, heard what had happened to their new neighbor. As the *New York*

Times reporter Nicholas Kristof tells it, during their Sunday worship service their pastor Chris George brought up their Muslim neighbor's plight and at the end of his sermon said, "Let's shower our neighbor with love."

More than two hundred members drove over to assist, mostly by making purchases. One man drove his car around until the gas tank was empty, so he could buy more gas.

"Our faith inspires us to build bridges, not to label people as *us* and *them*, but to recognize that we're all part of the same family," the pastor told the reporter. "Our world is a stronger place when we choose to look past labels and embrace others with love."

Good people, like the Smoke Rise Baptist Church, are reweaving our nation's social fabric even as it is being torn.[19]

Spiritual Exercise: Two Dimensions of Work

For Teilhard, the two main purposes of human effort are self-development and active work to contribute to God's project. For Teilhard, the two purposes are closely related. How can your self-development enrich your work for God's project? Give examples.

Called to Make Positive Change Happen

Everyone, working alone or together, has the power to make a difference. For example, even a group of high school girls from a poor and impoverished neighborhood can effect positive change.

Curtis Bay, a section of Baltimore, ranks as the most polluted area in the state of Maryland. Residents there are plagued with asthma. A young teen, Destiny Watford, and some fellow high school students heard that the state was planning to build what would have been the largest incinerator on the East Coast in their backyard. Destiny decided to lead a group of teenagers in a movement to stop this project.

"People thought our fight to stop the incinerator was a cute after-school hobby," she said. Rather, "It was an act of survival." She and her teen team "knocked on doors, pressed elected officials and confronted corporate executives until authorities revoked the project's permit," wrote a *TIME* magazine reporter.[20]

These youngsters had faced a huge challenge to change the way people perceived the incinerator's effects. Instead of seeing it as a project bringing in new jobs and more tax revenue to the state, they got the people in charge to realize that the project would destroy the health of young and old people in that area. And they succeeded.

"For so long our voice has been taken away from us or hindered in some way," Destiny Watford explained. "In creating our own narrative, we take the power back."[21]

Teilhard would have applauded the efforts of these youngsters, since his primary moral focus is on positive action, moving the evolutionary process forward. In his approach to moral living, he is much more intent on creating goodness than on avoiding traditional sins. These young people were positively motivated. They were intent on preserving their own health and that of their neighbors.

I'm sure many of their fellow teens felt they had no power to make change happen, and so opted to be indifferent or resigned to the incinerator's harmful effects. They would simply focus on enjoying what they could of their teen years. But Destiny Watford and her team realized they had the power to do something good for their community. And they did it. They took their power back. They owned it and used it.

The sins that concern Teilhard the most are sins of omission, things we could have done that would have furthered the kingdom of God, and we chose *not* to do them. In contrast, he would have us look for—even invent—positive things we can do to help God's project. He would have loved Destiny Watford and her friends for finding a new way to make a positive difference.

In America during the early days of the twentieth century, Roman Catholics, especially immigrants from Ireland and Europe, were unwelcome and even hated by many Americans, even though they immigrated legally. Once settled on our shores, they faced rejection, ridicule, and alienation. So, they often created ghettos where they enjoyed mutual protection. They took the most menial jobs.

Yet, during the next four or five decades, even while these unwelcome immigrants were struggling to survive, they managed to transform America. They built hundreds of magnificent churches across the land. They developed an unrivaled high-quality school system that taught tens of millions of immigrant children. Theirs were the children they sent to a newly built system of Catholic colleges and universities. There they trained to become doctors, lawyers, dentists, engineers, scientists, nurses, and teachers. They were proving the tremendous power of collective action and perseverance.

These same poor immigrant Catholics with their congregations of religious women also built and staffed hundreds of private hospitals across the country. These hospitals run by nuns rivaled, and often surpassed in quality, those supported by federal and state funding. Catholics in communities across the country promoted social justice; they backed the formation of workers' unions; they pushed for welfare reform. All of these were acts of boldness and daring carried out by mostly unwelcomed immigrants. What creativity! What ingenuity! What faith in God and in each other! They offer a stunning example of *each person taking positive action to make a positive difference, alone and with others.*

Although Catholic sisters, brothers, and priests started Catholic schools, colleges, and hospitals during the twentieth century primarily for the benefit of their fellow Catholics, they opened the doors of their institutions to anyone. Protestants, Jews, Hindus. Parents of other religions from Southeast Asia sent their children to Catholic schools and colleges because they recognized the high quality of the education and training in self-discipline they would receive there.[22] These same non-Catholics went to Catholic hospitals as patients because of the quality of medical and personal care they knew they would receive there.

But evolution moved on. Catholic schools and hospitals were no longer on the forefront of evolution. Many of these schools have disappeared and Catholic hospitals have been taken over and run by the government or for-profit organizations. What is called for today is not to open more traditional schools and hospitals, but to envision, invent, and create whatever is the next step needed in the evolutionary process.

More than ever, God is inspiring people to make changes that will help transform our planet and make our world a better place. The "divine presence underlying evolution demands to be clearly recognized as an ultimate and constant support for action."[23]

Teilhard reminds believers that God's project is the most important ongoing event happening during our lifetime and on this planet. Making our contributions to that divine project is our most fundamental ethical responsibility. Focusing on one's personal safety and security and merely avoiding traditional sins is not the response that God is looking for.

Transforming the planet with creativity, compassion, love, and a consciousness that embraces all things is our real job during our time

80

on Earth, not just getting through life and gaining heaven. To help make God's vision happen on Earth will take initiative, courage, and boldness.[24]

The institutional churches are not likely to take the initiative. Following their traditional modes of operating, the churches are more likely to play it safe, reinforce the rules and not take chances. Hopefully, members of congregations in small groups will. To take the needed evolutionary steps is up to individuals and small groups who are committed to transforming the world.

Often governments won't take the initiative. So, individuals and groups need to step forward. For example, when Congress cut NASA's budget, a bold and daring individual stood up. Space Exploration Technologies Corporation, better known as SpaceX, is an American aerospace manufacturer and space transportation company founded by a privately funded entrepreneur, Elon Musk. When Congress cut NASA's budget, Musk made it his goal to reduce space transportation costs. His larger vision involves colonizing Mars. People snickered at him. In the meantime, his company has produced launch vehicles for space travel that are designed to be recovered and reused, an accomplishment NASA never succeeded in doing. His cargo vehicle was the first privately owned liquid-propellant rocket to deliver supplies to the International Space Station.

Even in the everyday world, if you try to do something revolutionary, or merely out of the ordinary, you can expect plenty of critics, complainers, bystanders, cynics, protesters, and the like—even persecutors. They will try to instill doubt in you. Instead of spending your energy defending yourself, let them make their noise. Just move forward, focusing your energy on ways that you can make a positive difference. Stay focused on what's possible and go for it.[25] If you envision something that will make a difference, don't ask *Why?* and look for reasons to walk away from your vision. Rather, say *Why not?*

If you are starting a project that will bring new knowledge, new consciousness, more compassion into the world, don't debate with the atheist at your side about whether or not God is behind it. That's probably a waste of time. *You* know that God is behind it. That's all that counts. Better to enlist the atheist in your project by showing how your plan is something that will benefit everyone.

God wants to enlist everyone, even nonbelievers, in helping keep the God project going forward and upward. You do not have to use

81

God language or religious concepts to sell your idea. It is enough for you to show that it is helping build a more loving and conscious planet. That will be enough to promote it among nonbelievers.

Francis Collins, the physician who oversaw the government's project to map the human genome, happens to be a devout Christian. He knew that this genetic map would move the evolutionary process forward in many ways. Although Dr. Collins saw the human genome as "God's language" and a kind of divine revelation, he did not make believing in God a condition for anyone working on the project. He knew that everyone understood that the mapping of the human genome was a forward step in science and medicine. They would be committed to it simply for the many benefits it would bring to humanity.[26]

Spiritual Exercise: Powerless?

How can people overcome the belief that they can't change the way things are? What can we learn from each of these few examples to help people overcome their sense of powerlessness?

The Role of Prayer

In the traditional moral system, one of the best ways to avoid sin and temptation was to pray.[27] From this perspective, a vocation dedicated to contemplative prayer came to be considered the highest form of the spiritual life. The theory was that the more time you spent in prayer with God, the better. Moreover, increasing your prayer time meant the less time for you to be tempted to sin. That may or may not be true. However, most of us were not called to be cloistered nuns or hermit monks.

If we consider Jesus, he saw action, not prayer, as his primary responsibility. His mission in word and deed was to proclaim the presence of the kingdom of God in our midst. Of course, Jesus prayed privately, but one purpose of his private prayer, spending time with his Father, was to reconnect and reenergize him for his active mission.[28]

Another way to look at prayer in the context of Teilhard's call to action is to recall St. Ignatius of Loyola encouraging his fellow Jesuits to become "contemplatives in action." This meant that, even amid their daily activities, Jesuits were to learn to remain in God's presence.

Many saints in their journals comment on having this sense of God's presence in their work.

When St. Ignatius's Jesuits were starting a new and difficult ministry, such as setting up a new college or going on a faraway missionary journey, he would tell them to "pray as if everything depended on God, and act as if everything depended on you."

In this second ethical principle, Teilhard is telling us that the most important way for us to fulfill our promise to God, that is, when we say to God, "Thy will be done on Earth," is to take positive action to make a positive difference. Don't let your faults, failures, or sins stop you from going forward. No matter how often you fail, God still loves you unconditionally and encourages you to continue to do what you can.

An evolutionary ethics is focused on each person taking positive action to make a positive difference.

Spiritual Exercise: A New Positive Mindset

In the traditional approach to the moral life, fear was a strong motivator for avoiding sin and "being good." In this new mindset, hope, optimism, and confidence are the new motivators. How would making this emotional shift affect the way you currently live? Have you ever tried to do something good for the community that took courage and boldness?

ETHICAL PRINCIPLE 3:
Try Anything to Advance God's Project

The moral call is to be willing to try anything that offers hope for advancing God's project. *(Derived from Basic Principles 2, 3, 4, 6, 7, 8)*

The key words in this third principle are *to try anything that offers hope* for advancing God's project. In Teilhard's words, "To try everything for the sake of ever increasing knowledge and power: this is the most general formula and the highest law of human activity and morality."[29]

Recognizing the immense evolutionary task, Teilhard wrote, "It is eminently on this ground that we must try *everything*, to its conclusion."[30]

And on the very last page of *The Divine Milieu*, Teilhard cries out to his readers, "We must try everything for Christ; we must hope everything for Christ....That is the true Christian attitude."

When Teilhard says, "Be willing to try anything for Christ," he is talking about things that no one has yet envisioned, what no one else has created. No one can invent a smartphone app that will show people how to envision and create the future. Those creative visions are born in human hearts, minds, and imaginations.

At first glance, this principle may seem to apply only to people on the frontiers of science, medicine, and technology. We might spontaneously think of billionaires like Elon Musk that can create their own space program, or Dr. Francis Collins, who has a prominent position with the National Institutes of Health and has access to millions of dollars for human genome research—as if only powerful people can advance the consciousness of humanity. But Teilhard intended this moral guide for everyone. God has given talents to everyone that they can use in whatever ways are available to them.

The way to think about this principle is to begin by saying, "I would like to make a difference." Whatever action you do, if it is done with love and concern, *will* make a difference. In previous sections, we have seen ordinary people, despite their limitations, accomplish extraordinary things. Recall Destiny Watford and her high-school classmates who stopped a giant incinerator from being built in their neighborhood, or the thousands of poor Catholic immigrants, mostly unwelcomed when they arrived in America, who managed to build a mammoth high-quality parochial school system throughout the United States as well as a superb hospital system. Steve Jobs started as a kid tinkering with electronics in his parent's garage; he went on to create Apple Inc. and change the world of communication forever. Four kids from Liverpool started practicing in a family garage; as the Beatles, they went on to transform and evolve popular music. Teilhard's point is this: never underestimate what you can do to promote God's project. Making a difference begins with a vision and imagination.

Imagination is considered by some as the highest faculty in human consciousness. Imagination, they point out, is the only faculty that can integrate past, present, and future. Memory can't do that, neither can intellect or willpower. Imagination is the faculty that enables us to build upon the *past*, realize how far we have come in the *present*, and envision the *future*. Only imagination!

84

Imagination allows us to envision possibilities and expand our horizons. For example, for centuries, smallpox had been a scourge on the world, until Dr. Edward Jenner in 1796 envisioned and then discovered a vaccine to prevent it. By the 1960s, smallpox had been effectively eradicated in the United States. Dr. Donald Henderson (1927–2016), an American epidemiologist, held a grander vision for the future. He imagined ridding the entire world of smallpox. Starting in 1966, he led the World Health Organization's effort against the smallpox virus, and by 1980 the disease had been eradicated worldwide.[31]

For Teilhard, the next steps in each evolutionary process beyond the present are already in the air waiting to be recognized. He writes, "By virtue of a marvelous mounting force contained in things, each reality attained and left behind gives us access to the discovery and pursuit of an ideal of higher spiritual content."[32]

The law of evolution is always at work within everything and everyone. The more a person feels this evolutionary force within, according to Teilhard, "the more avid he becomes for great and sublime aims to pursue....He will want wider organizations to create, new paths to blaze, causes to uphold, truths to discover, an ideal to cherish and defend. So, gradually, the worker no longer belongs to himself. Little by little the great breath of the universe has insinuated itself into him."[33]

Teilhard encourages us to "love the invisible" and to "love the not-yet." Imagination enables us to "see" or envision the invisible and picture what has not-yet been created. Someone had to imagine the light bulb before it could be invented. Someone had to first imagine a building before it could be built. Someone had to imagine a new business before it could be set up. Someone had to imagine a spaceship landing on the moon. Someone had to imagine beginning a colony on Mars.

Teilhard wants us to use our imaginations to see the next step in the evolution of love and to help bring it about. Teilhard wants us to use our imaginations to find new ways of generating love. He encourages us to envision ways that we can possibly build the Body of Christ on our planet and to help renew the face of Earth.

In the early days of comic strips, there were cartoonists who envisioned the future. Back in the 1940s, I recall eagerly devouring daily newspaper comic strips of Buck Rogers's rocket ships going to the moon and other planets. During this same period, Chester Gould, the creator of the comic strip Dick Tracy, envisioned a smartphone worn on the wrist. There were science fiction writers like H. G. Wells who described submarines and submersible vehicles long before they were invented. Imagination remains a key faculty in future human evolution.

Spiritual Exercise: Using Your Imagination

To complete a new project that you have never attempted before involves much time and effort. It must begin with you imagining the desired outcome. Imagination is required before you can take the first action steps. Can you name a situation or challenge where your imagination proved helpful in accomplishing a challenging task?

Beyond a Sure Thing

Suppose there is something you are certain will advance God's project, and you are invited to do it or to get involved with those who are doing it. That is *not* what Teilhard is talking about in this third ethical principle. What you have been invited into is a "sure thing." This principle goes far beyond getting involved in a sure thing. Rather, it puts us in the realm of the untried, the domain of things that have never been envisioned.

Or, suppose you are invited to participate in a new project whose results or effects cannot be predicted. In other words, this novel project might or might not advance God's project, but you will never know until you try it.[34] This is the kind of enterprise that Teilhard is talking about in this principle.

It is a very daring moral principle, since Teilhard is asking us to be willing to try an "unsure thing": something that might not work, or might be ethically questionable, or might have ethically questionable elements as part of it, or might produce negative effects as well as positive ones. Or, it may fail to produce any visible effects at all.

Sometimes, we try with all our strength and perseverance to get a great idea off the ground, but it just doesn't happen. I know of a couple, Rose and Dan Lucey, who lobbied Congress for many years to start a National Peace Academy. The Luceys began trying in the 1950s and continued well into the 1970s. Their hope was that the government would recognize the need for such a school. They felt that, in addition to the number of military academies that Congress financed to train young men and women to conduct strategies for war, our nation deserved to have at least one government-sponsored National Peace Academy that officially trained men and women in the strategies of peacemaking.

The Luceys' quest never succeeded. They never saw their idea get off the ground. Instead, sadly, they saw the government create the School of the Americas. At this "school," American experts in guerrilla tactics, psychological warfare, and techniques of torture trained South American and Central American military leaders in these vicious practices. The government was more interested in supporting a school that taught the ways of warfare rather than of peacemaking. Yet the Luceys never stopped trying, never stopped holding a vision of a peace academy.

Sometimes scientists are faced with ethically questionable actions. Albert Einstein, a world-famous physicist, considered himself to be a pacifist. In 1929, he publicly declared that if a war broke out he would "unconditionally refuse to do war service, direct or indirect...regardless of how the cause of the war should be judged." Yet he did participate in World War II. Though Einstein was not directly involved in the invention of the atomic bomb, he was instrumental in encouraging its development. His role in the invention of the atomic bomb involved merely signing a letter to President Franklin Roosevelt urging that the bomb be built. Nothing else. He wavered before he took his pen in hand because he knew his signature would make a significant difference in Roosevelt's decision. He finally did it because he feared that Hitler's Nazi scientists might already be developing such a weapon.

Even in signing the letter, he recognized future problems that such weapons could bring. He wrote to physicist Niels Bohr in December 1944, "When the war is over, then there will be in all countries a pursuit of secret war preparations with technological means which will lead inevitably to preventative wars and to destruction even more terrible than the present destruction of life."

In November 1954, five months before his death, Einstein summarized his feelings about his role in the creation of the atomic bomb: "I made one great mistake in my life...when I signed the letter to President Roosevelt recommending that atom bombs be made; but there was some justification—the danger that the Germans would make them."[35]

In the following years, Einstein's predictions came true as the United States and the USSR ran a race to see who would be able to accumulate the biggest nuclear arsenal.

At the same time, atomic energy did prove to have many benefits outside of warfare. Today, atomic energy, also referred to as nuclear energy, is used to generate electricity for many communities. What most people don't know is that nuclear energy also has applications in the fields of agriculture, medicine, research, and industry. This energy contains highly active radioisotopes, which makes it suitable for different chemical, electrical, engineering, and industrial practices. Atomic energy is used today to generate fertilizers and to increase genetic variability of plants and crops such as sorghum, bananas, beans, wheat, and peppers. Atomic energy also facilitates insect control. And it is used in the field of medicine, too, where it is added to diagnostic equipment and compounds. Atomic energy also sees widespread use in the environmental field, where it is added to tracers to detect and analyze pollutants.

There are times in life when each of us is faced with getting involved in projects that are ethically questionable. The challenge is to discern whether the possible positive benefits of the project outweigh the possible negative ones.

Teilhard sets no limits on what we should try for Christ, even if we fail or get ourselves muddied up in the process. Throughout *The Divine Milieu*, Teilhard explores the darker side of the consequences of our actions that are done with the best of intentions.[36] Working for scientific, religious, community, or political development may even involve getting into trouble. We may stand in a picket line for a cause we believe in; or walk in a protest march; or write letters, articles, or books that challenge the status quo. Even if we may be rejected, punished, or persecuted for our attempt, Teilhard said, we should still try it. "We must test every barrier, try every path, plumb every abyss. Leave nothing untried....God wills it, and willed that he should have need of it."[37] Teilhard certainly knew rejection for trying something new for Christ.

Traditionally, the moral rule was to play it safe, avoid the messiness of involvement in anything that might be ethically questionable. It was strongly suggested that such activity would only sully your soul. If you must be involved in "the world," traditional morality said, keep your secular life separate from your spiritual life. It emphasized that they were two different realms.

For example, in Teilhard's time, if you had been a priest educated as a scientist, you were to act as a scientist while you were in a classroom or a laboratory. When you left your secular work, however, you were expected to close the curtain on your professional life for that day and return to your room and your sacred work, such as prayer and worship. Such a person was called a priest-scientist. He lived a "hyphenated" life. He was to keep his two roles separate, and to remember that his prayer life was most important. He was reminded by the church, "God is interested only in your spiritual life. That is your real work. Your scientific pursuits are merely secular and ultimately unimportant to God. Only your eternal salvation is."[38]

In contrast, for Teilhard, every person's moral life is centered on helping build the Body of Christ. And since that function involves moving forward in all aspects of life, Christians are called to plunge into life in whatever field of endeavor they happen to be.[39] For him, it is "the sense of the mutual completion of the world and God which gives life to Christianity."[40] For Teilhard, there is no real distinction between the sacred and the secular. Many so-called secular occupations are, in fact, helping build unity and health in the Body of Christ. Your "secular" work is ultimately important to God, because it is your personal context for helping develop the Body of Christ.

Like Ignatius Loyola, his spiritual leader, Teilhard tells us to ask ourselves, "What can I do for Christ?" "What am I not doing that I could be doing for Christ?"

We are all involved in Christogenesis—bringing the universal or Cosmic Christ to his fullest maturity. The word *genesis*, as in *Christogenesis*, refers to something that is still in the process of becoming what it is meant to be. A baby in the womb we say is "gestating." It is in its genesis. It's still in the process of developing its full human form and functions. As the human family, we are all still in a "genesis" process, personally and in Christ. We are still becoming what we were meant to be and working to accomplish what we were meant to accomplish. As each of us becomes more developed, mature, and "ripe," humanity is becoming more capable of participating in Christ's own fullness and development, that is, in Christogenesis. For Teilhard, Christogenesis is another way of talking about God's project, since God's project is to bring the Cosmic Christ to his fullest maturity.

Each of us has unique contributions to make to that divine project. We do bits of evolutionary work each day in our interactions with people and in our jobs. What we are called to do in our daily work and relationships is not just see ourselves as doing some merely human work. Our daily work is important, because it is part of a much bigger project. Our purpose while on Earth, Teilhard said, "is not simply to forward a human task but to bring Christ to completion."[41] It is to participate in God's project. All such work that we do is sacred.

The word *sacred* is no longer necessary, says Teilhard, because in Christogenesis—or God's project—there is really no distinction between sacred and secular. For Teilhard, the adjective *sacred* can be applied in the realm of food production, comedy shows, or transportation, as long as it builds connections, unity, and love.

Clarence Birdseye knew that existing freezing methods were inferior and led to bland-tasting reheated food. He envisioned and developed quick-freeze machinery to produce quality frozen food. Shoppers didn't believe him. Clarence Birdseye went broke. He stuck with it, eventually overcame consumer skepticism, and went on to set the industry standard in Birdseye frozen foods.

Television network executives in the 1970s weren't sure the viewing public would accept a sitcom with a Cuban leading man married to a feisty American redhead. So Desi Arnaz and Lucille Ball produced the *I Love Lucy* pilot with their own money. Network executives said television shows had to be produced in New York using kinescopes. Lucy and Desi took a salary cut to produce the show in Hollywood on expensive film. But, as part of the deal, the couple kept rights to the show. At every turn, Lucy and Desi were a step ahead of the studios, revolutionizing television along the way.

While attending Yale University in the mid-1960s, Fred Smith wrote an economics term paper on the need for a reliable overnight delivery service in a computerized information age. His professor was less than impressed with Smith's paper and responded, "The concept is interesting and well-formed, but in order to earn a grade better than a 'C,' the idea must be feasible." Years later, many potential investors agreed with the skeptical professor, refusing to send Smith any capital. The funds he managed to raise in 1971 and '72 were gone by '74, along with his investors. Nevertheless, through a combination of innovative thinking, unbridled charisma, and sheer determination, Smith would use this "interesting but unfeasible" concept to establish the world's first overnight delivery company we today call FedEx. One catchy slogan — *Whatever It Takes!* — and several million dollars of hard-won capital later, Federal Express was on its way to profitability and long-term success. He changed the transportation industry forever.

As this ethical principle says, *the moral call is to be willing to try anything that offers hope for advancing God's project.* Stories of success remind us not to give up hope.

One last clarification. Teilhard is not trying to make you feel guilty if you do not try to do something extraordinary. Quite the opposite. He is inviting you *to think of yourself in a new way:* as someone with imagination and creativity that can make a positive difference.

Spiritual Exercise: Willing to Try

Have you ever been invited to join a group or become part of a project where you were unsure that the outcome would be something good and useful for building community? How did you deal with that invitation? Do you think Teilhard would like that slogan, Whatever it Takes!?

ETHICAL PRINCIPLE 4:
Two Primary Ethical Responsibilities

Two primary ethical responsibilities shared by every person are (1) to build and maintain an ever-expanding loving human community and (2) to care for the health and welfare of the planet (to love matter). No one is excused from these responsibilities. *(Derived from Basic Principles 5, 6, 7, 8)*

In a traditional ethical system, one's responsibilities are, simply, to save one's soul. Because there is no other religious expectation than personal salvation, there is no clear moral or ethical requirement that we expand the reach of our love beyond our families and neighbors. A more expansive love may be encouraged, but it is not required, nor is there a requirement that we develop an ecological conscience, since people in this traditional moral framework believe we are on Earth only as temporary "visitors." Some popular prayers even refer to Earth as a "valley of tears" or "our exile."

91

Regarding the first responsibility, *to build and maintain an ever-expanding loving community among humans,* we are challenged to embrace more and more people in our lives, not just our family and friends.

Even the smallest gesture has impact. If you are like me, I typically carry a few dollar bills with me for the homeless. I used to just hand a dollar to a homeless person and keep going. But someone told me a better way. When you hand your gift to the needy person, ask the person their name and tell them your first name. If appropriate, shake hands too. Make a point to say their name out loud and wish them a blessing. That way, you will have made a small personal connection. You have brought the world a tiny bit closer together in love.

Gestures made together with others can have an even larger impact. There are many opportunities for people to learn how to connect with each other and work together on a project.

Habitat for Humanity is an organization operating across the United States that brings together groups of people who work together to achieve an objective. In this case, the task is to build a home for someone who can't afford it. As its home page states, "At Habitat for Humanity, we build because we believe that everyone, everywhere, should have a healthy, affordable place to call home. More than building homes, we build communities, we build hope and we build the opportunity for families to help themselves."[42]

For example, in Tampa, Florida, employees and managers from the Tampa Honda dealership mobilized a team of workers to help build a new three-bedroom home for Pricilla Pate, a single mother. When the home was built and ready, Mary Hutton, a Habitat for Humanity volunteer, presented the participant workers with symbolic hammers and commented on the shared bond that the hammers represent:

> Habitat is a partnership founded on common ground—bridging theological differences by putting love into action. While we acknowledge that we may disagree on many things, we agree that everyone can use the hammer as an instrument to manifest God's love. Habitat's late founder, Miller Fuller, called this concept the "theology of the hammer."
>
> "The Bible teaches that God is the God of the whole crowd," said Fuller. God's love leaves nobody out, and [our] love should not either. This understanding drives

Eleven Principles of Teilhard's Ethics

"the theology of the hammer" which empowers each of us to build together with our brothers and sisters who need affordable housing.

Celebrating with the crowd of workers, Ms. Pate [the new homeowner] expressed her gratitude to everyone who helped make the home possible. "I would like to thank everyone who helped make my dream come true."[43]

This is just one example of many ways to build and maintain an ever-expanding loving community among humans. In this story, the employees at Tampa Honda that helped build Pricilla Pate's home may never have had the chance to work side by side inside the Honda dealership building. The sales team never got to work side by side with the auto repair department, or with the parts department, or with the financial department. But in building the home for Pricilla Pate they did. And they all got to know Pricilla and her children. In this way, the employees and managers at Tampa Honda became a loving community, not merely employees of different departments.

Sometimes it is difficult to get members of a community to meet one another.

Most people are familiar with the story of the Good Samaritan, but here is a more modern one about breakfast at McDonald's told by a mother of three children. The mother had just finished her college degree:

The last class I had to take was sociology. The teacher was absolutely inspiring....Her last project of the term was called, "Smile." The class was asked to go out, smile at three people, and document their reactions.

I am a very friendly person, and I always smile at everyone and say hello, so I thought this would be a piece of cake. Soon after we were assigned the project, my husband, youngest son, and I went out to McDonald's one crisp March morning. It was our way of sharing special playtime with our son. We were standing in line, waiting to be served, when all of a sudden everyone around us began to back away—even my husband. I did not move an inch. An overwhelming feeling of panic welled up inside of me as I turned to see why they had moved.

As I turned around, I smelled a horrible, dirty body smell, and there, standing behind me, were two poor homeless men. As I looked down at the short gentleman standing closer to me, he was smiling. His beautiful sky blue eyes were full of God's light as he searched for acceptance. He said, "Good day," as he counted the few coins he had been clutching.

The second man fumbled with his hands as he stood behind his friend. I realized the second man was mentally challenged and that the blue-eyed gentleman was his salvation.

I held my tears as I stood there with them. The young lady at the counter asked him what they wanted.

He said, "Coffee is all, Miss," because that was all they could afford. (If they wanted to sit in the restaurant and warm up, they had to buy something. He just wanted to be warm).

Then I really felt it—the compulsion was so great I almost reached over and embraced the little man with the blue eyes. That is when I noticed all eyes in the restaurant were set on me, judging my every action. I smiled and asked the young lady behind the counter to give me two more breakfast meals on a separate tray. I then walked around the corner to the table that the men had chosen as a resting spot. I put the tray on the table and laid my hand on the blue-eyed gentleman's cold hand.

He looked up at me, with tears in his eyes, and said, "Thank you."

I leaned over, began to pat his hand and said, "I did not do this for you. God is here working through me to give you hope." I started to cry as I walked away to join my husband and son. When I sat down, my husband smiled at me and said, "That is why God gave you to me, Honey. To give me hope."

We held hands for a moment and, at that time; we knew that only because of the grace that we had been given were we able to give.[++]

There is probably no decent person who couldn't see themselves in this woman's shoes. Because of the grace we were given, we can give.

Moses reminded the people that they all have the power to show God's love to one another. He says to the people,

> Surely, this commandment [of love] that I am command- ing you today is not too hard for you, nor is it too far away. It is not in heaven, that you should say, "Who will go up to heaven for us, and get it for us so that we may hear it and observe it?" Neither is it beyond the sea, that you should say, "Who will cross to the other side of the sea for us, and get it for us so that we may hear it and observe it?" No, the word is very near to you; it is in your mouth and in your heart for you to observe. (Deut 30:11–14)

In his parable of the Good Samaritan (see Luke 10:25–37), Jesus is merely repeating what Moses said. This law of love is something very near to you. It is already in your mouths and written in your hearts. The Samaritan man felt it and acted upon it. The priest and Levite in the story most likely felt it too but refused to act upon it.

Teilhard might say, "Do you want to know how to make a positive difference? All you have to do is act upon what is already in your heart."

When Jacob Cramer was ten years old, he lost his grandfather. "Missing him, he began to deliver greetings to residents of a nursing home near his Cleveland home. He's grown that act of kindness into Love for the Elderly, a nonprofit that has collected more than 15,000 anonymous letters from 51 countries and given them to senior citizens nationwide." Jacob, now sixteen, says, "It makes me so happy to give out these letters and see the smiles the seniors have when they open the envelope."[45]

In 2017, the editors of *Parade* magazine, along with Random Acts of Kindness Foundation, sponsored "a year of taking kindness to the streets." "Do one simple act of kindness each day of the year" was their motto. If you needed ideas, they recommended several books and orga- nizations.

Spiritual Exercise: Today's Good Samaritans

Is it so hard to show love to someone you don't know? Or don't like? Must we always be like the priest and the Levite who avoided the wounded man? Must we always be like the others in the McDonald's story who walked away from the men whose body odor they found offensive? Is it so hard to show a little love to someone you don't know?

Caring for Our Planet

—— The second responsibility listed in this ethical principle is *to care for the health and welfare of the planet.* Or, as Teilhard would put it, *to love matter.*

We who are very conscious of today's ecological crisis must remember that Teilhard lived and died before scientists became aware of the precarious state of our planet. In the indexes of Teilhard's books and collections of essays, one looks in vain for terms like *ecology* or *the environment.* In his day, people had never heard of global warming, rising sea levels, melting icebergs, carbon footprints, toxic chemicals and industrial wastes polluting rivers and lakes, millions of tons of non-biodegradable plastic containers dumped in the ocean, and so on. His generation could never imagine that, today, Americans—in homes, supermarkets, and restaurants—throw away up to 40 percent of consumable foods.

However, through the media today, we are made very conscious of the urgent need to care for our Earth and of what we have been doing to ruin it.

Teilhard loved Earth passionately, especially its future. But to find the roots of Teilhard's ecological sensitivity, one must look more deeply into his thought. For example, in his day Teilhard was aware of a new "element" of humanity that was popping up all over the noosphere. In 1945, he wrote of this new element: "We might call it *Homo progressivus* (man of progress), that is to say, the man to whom the terrestrial future matters more than [to most people at] present."[46] "When we come to look for them, men of this sort are easily recognizable," says Teilhard. "They are scientists, thinkers, airmen [astronauts], and so on—all those possessed by the demon (or angel) of Research."[47] For him, the men and women who love Earth's future manifest the spirit of evolution.

Theologically, because of his Judeo-Christian orientation, Teilhard knew that everything God created was good and lovable. Jesus emphasized the divine love for creation in his late-night dialogue with Nicodemus (see John 3). At one point in the conversation, Jesus said —— to Nicodemus, "For God so loved the world that he gave his only Son, so that everyone who believes in him may not perish but may have eternal life" (John 3:16). People tend to read the expression "God so loved the world" as if "the world" referred simply to humanity. The original Greek text is clear. It says, "God so loved the *cosmos*..."—all of creation, not just humans.

Then, to make sure Nicodemus got the point, Jesus added, "Indeed, God did not send the Son into the world to condemn the world, but in order that the world [all creation] might be saved through him" (John 3:17). The word *saved* has a special meaning for Jesus. For him, to be saved—or *salvation*—means having or enjoying the fullness of life.[48] God wants all of nature to enjoy the fullness of life. St. Paul is clear that God's project involves all creation, not merely the human family.[49] This is ecological.

Biologists tell us that our planet is really one immense biological and ecological organism. Everyone is inextricably intertwined with every other element of Earth, and with the continuing health of this planetary organism. Teilhard knew this. In the incarnation, the Son of God—a divine Person—in a supreme act of love and self-emptying became an integral part of this immense planetary organism.[50] Jesus of Nazareth had lungs that breathed our atmosphere; he had a heart that pumped blood with a certain blood type; he had a bladder and bowels that needed to be relieved from time to time; he had a stomach filled with bacteria to help him digest food; he had a voice to share conversation with others; and he had a mind that processed ideas. He had fingers and toes, a back that sometimes got sore, skin that could sweat. He would bleed if he got cut; he would feel hurt if someone insulted him. In a word, he was human like us.

For Teilhard, the incarnation of Jesus Christ became the tangible guarantee of God's love, not only for humankind, but also for all of nature. When the incarnation is truly understood, Teilhard felt, the distinctions between sacred and secular, matter and spirit—two ancient dualisms—no longer provide an appropriate basis of theology and spirituality. Because of the incarnation, the divine is permanently immersed in Earth. The sacred and spiritual cannot be separated from the secular and material.

Because of this intimate God-Earth connection, Teilhard said, people, especially Christians, were called both to love God passionately and to love the world passionately. Because God still loves this evolving world as much as God still loves his divine Son (John 3:16),

Teilhard would say, we are called to love the planet and be committed to furthering its evolution.

Once we accept the universal scope of God's project, it becomes an obvious responsibility not only to continue expanding the breadth and depth of our love to include all human beings, but also to devote ourselves to caring for the planet. The Bible has always presented Earth as our common home and life source.[51]

As Pope Francis pointed out in his encyclical on ecology, *Laudato Sí*, just as we can sin against humans by failing to love and care for them, so we can sin against the environment by not loving it and failing to manage its resources in ways that foster the fullness of life for all.

The significant subtitle of the pope's new encyclical is "On Care of Our Common Home." The implication is that Earth is humanity's home and all its riches belong to everyone, not just the wealthy nations and rich people. Earth is not a place of exile, as some traditional prayers suggest, but our home. Therefore, we should care passionately about its health.[52]

Here's a very quick, four-step summary of the pope's thinking on our common home, the Earth:

Fact One: Every day we say the Lord's Prayer and in it we promise God that we will do what God wants us to do on Earth. "Thy will be done on Earth." That's our promise.

Fact Two: We are slowly exploiting and ruining this common home that God gave us to care for.

Fact Three: On polluting our earth and its atmosphere, the pope says we have invented new ways to sin against the home God gave us. We are violating the environment, our home. We humans, individually and collectively, are committing sins against the environment.

Fact Four: As far as the pope is concerned, the worst sin against the environment is to realize how our Earth is being destroyed *and to do nothing about it*.

In other words, we just keep behaving as if there is nothing wrong. And even if there was something wrong, we say we can do nothing about it. We blame others for the dire situation, excusing ourselves by saying that we as individuals can do nothing or claiming that we are not responsible.

But there are many who accept their responsibility. From Francis's point of view, small and local is beautiful: "In some places," he writes, "cooperatives are being developed to exploit renewable sources of energy which ensure local self-sufficiency and even the sale of surplus energy." Ursula Sladek is the one who sparked the energy revolution in Germany by helping transform her hometown — the town of Schönau — from energy dependence.

There are cities and towns in Germany, like Schönau, that have created their own electrical power grid because the solar energy produced by solar panels on the roofs of almost every home in the town generates more energy than the people in that town need. They send extra electrical energy to the grid so that other places that need energy can tap into it. These towns have made themselves self-sufficient for electrical energy. They even generate more than needed. This simple example shows that, while the existing world order of nations may prove powerless to assume its responsibilities, local individuals and groups can make a real difference.

A native of Liberia, Africa, Saran Kaba Jones, in her early thirties, returned to her homeland after many years abroad. She was unprepared for the wreckage she found there after years of civil war. "I had seen it on TV," she said, "but seeing kids on the street, selling snacks to support their families instead of going to school, that made it real." Her first plan was to spend a month launching an educational scholarship fund and leave Liberia knowing she had done something for her people.

"I went thinking education was the solution, but when I talked to people, it was water, water, water." Most rural areas had no access to clean running water, and kids were missing school, so they could haul water home. So, Kaba Jones refocused her efforts on building water systems for rural areas in Liberia. She started an organization named FACE Africa. In its first seven years, FACE built over fifty water systems, all of which are still in operation. She had to figure out how to make those systems last, so her organization also trained local technicians on how to repair any problems.[53]

Climate change is another major area of global concern where individuals can help with research. In Alaska, for example, native teens are helping scientists contribute to research about global warming.

Students learn to use both native and Western perspectives of nature to better understand global warming and its consequences. For example, native students working alongside scientists study the relationship between climate change and the functions of lake ice and snow. They examine how lakes store solar energy and how measurements of snow density, ice thickness, thermal conductivity, and temperature gradients provide information about climate. Working outdoors, the students learn why it is important to study changes in the environment—such as the transition of tundra to boreal forest—and how the changes may affect the way of life in local communities, and how these communities will need to find ways to adapt.[54]

Waste of resources is another issue where individuals and small groups can make a difference.

Leon was retired but he got restless in retirement and wanted to do something helpful and meaningful. He lived in Seattle, Washington. One of his neighbors who worked in the janitorial service of a big office tower casually mentioned to Leon that they threw away half-used rolls of toilet paper. The neighbor explained that it was company policy that when a roll of toilet paper was near half used, the janitors were to remove it and insert a new, full roll of toilet paper.

Leon got permission to gather the half-used rolls from the cleaning crew. He then delivered them to a local food bank. The people there would distribute them to the poor. Leon then began going to different office buildings to gather the half-used rolls of toilet paper. He's been doing this now for about fifteen years. He has given the poor more than the equivalent of one million full rolls of toilet paper. When he was asked about this service that he had invented, Leon said, "To me it just seemed like a nice thing to do for others."

Sometimes we forget that we share this planet with many animals. And with our pets we often share our homes.

Connor McCannon is an eighth grader at the La Crosse Design Institute at Longfellow Middle School. He volunteers at least once a week at the Coulee Region Humane Society, working with the dogs as they wait to be adopted. He plays and socializes with them, making sure they get their exercise.

Connor says that he volunteers his time simply because he loves to do it. "The dogs just love to see me every day, and they don't get that much attention. As long as I can keep them happy until they get adopted, that's just all that counts. You get to see different animals every day, and once you see an animal not there, you know it's been adopted and you can't help to smile to know how good they're doing now."

Connor is one of about 375 volunteers at the humane society in his town, but the volunteer coordinator says Connor's been making an impact since almost the day he started. "Connor is just a fantastic volunteer overall, he's so kind, so polite, he's here with a smile on his face every time, and I think his enthusiasm is what makes him just a spectacular volunteer," said Rebecca Rowe.

Connor says his favorite breed to work with at the humane society is pit bulls. He says if they weren't so misunderstood, more of them would be adopted.[55]

Spiritual Exercise: God Plants Love Seeds in Us

God plants "love seeds" in each of us, as in Jesus's parable of the sower (see Matt 13:1–8). These seeds are meant to grow in us and produce output. In the parable, some of the seeds fall by the wayside or in thorns and don't produce much. In the story, the love seed God planted in Leon was quite productive. Leon felt restless and wanted to do something to make a difference. God's seed in Leon was sparked by a friend who told him about large office buildings wasting toilet paper. Do you have some seeds that God has planted in you that have yet to produce results? Do you know of other stories like that of Leon's where God's seeds have borne good results?

ETHICAL PRINCIPLE 5:
Nurturing the Evolutionary Process

Each one, according to his or her resources of love energy, is morally obliged to nurture the evolutionary process. *(Derived from Basic Principles 2, 4, 5, 6, 7, 8)*

This is a principle about using one's resources, specifically love energy. Here, Teilhard is telling us that each person—no exceptions—has a moral obligation to try to make a positive difference in the world using whatever loving resources they have. The emphasis is on nurturing the evolutionary process, doing your part for the success of God's project.

In this principle, Teilhard is helping people overcome the classic dualism of traditional theology, morality and spirituality. Theologian Robert Faricy describes the apparent self-contradiction in this dualism:

> Christianity is plagued by a spiritual dualism, by a conflict between the Church's teaching on the Christian duty to work and the notion that the world is vanity. It is one thing to point out that there is a divine precept to labor and to develop the earth. But if it is immediately added that the results of that labor are perishable and useless, that the world is given to man just as a spinwheel is put in a squirrel's cage, chiefly to help him to exercise and go through the motions of living, how can man have any enthusiasm for his work or for life itself? For man to give himself wholeheartedly to the work of the universe, he must be convinced not only of the merit of what he does, but of its value. He needs to believe in what he is doing.[56]

Teilhard would never want you to read this fifth principle and feel guilty that you have not used every ounce of your abilities to accomplish everything you do perfectly. Nor would he expect multitalented persons to develop fully every one of their talents. Albert Einstein, the foremost physicist of the twentieth century, also had musical talent. Though he loved performing on his violin, music took a place of lesser importance in his life. What was important was that he used his abilities to contribute to the world. Teilhard wants to wake us up to the significance of using our opportunities to make a difference. Don't be afraid to try something new, to experiment, to test your ideas, to see if they work. If God has a project going on, helping that project move forward is why you were created.

No one is excused from this assignment. No "buts" are allowed. You cannot say, "But I'm afraid I might fail," or "But I am not very good at it," or "But I am sick and dying," or "But I am poor," or "But I am mentally ill," or "But I am wheelchair bound," or "But I am an orphan," or "But I am an addict," or "But I was severely abused as a child," or "But I am a sinful person," or "But I quit going to church," or "But I am in prison," or "But I don't believe in God."

Author and lecturer Matthew Kelly reminds us that the simple basic requirement for helping build God's project is to make yourself available:

> For thousands of years, God has been using ordinary people
> to do extraordinary things. He delights in dynamic collab-
> oration with humanity. He doesn't necessarily choose the
> people who are the best educated or who are good-looking;
> he doesn't choose people because they are in positions of
> power and authority; he doesn't always choose the most elo-
> quent or persuasive. There is only one type of person God
> has used throughout history; He does incredible things with
> the people who make themselves available to him; it is the
> prerequisite for mission.[57]

Everyone has resources of love energy. Matthew Kelly tells this story about his own discovery of love energy:

> Before I became a father, I thought I knew something about
> the love God the Father has for me. Then my son Walter
> was born. I found myself constantly yearning to be with
> him. He couldn't walk or talk. All he did was eat, and sleep,
> and need his diaper changed. But I loved being with him.
>   Over the years, that hasn't changed. As my wife and I
> have had more children, I yearn to be with each of them in
> the same way. I love my children so much it's crazy, really.
> And before I had them I just didn't understand. But as I
> began to think about this great love I have for my children,
> the love of God took on a whole new meaning. Because if I
> can love my children as much as I do, and I am broken and
> wounded and flawed and limited, imagine how much God
> loves us. This thought was overwhelming to me and took my
> relationship with God to the next level.[58]

Love energy is much more than showing affection and saying, "I love you." Love energy includes using one's imagination, creativity, innovation, research, discovery, and collaboration with others in all fields of endeavor to foster renewal of the face of the Earth. You can also foster creativity in others, as Thomas Edison's mother did.

One day, Thomas Edison came home from primary school and gave a note to his mother. He told her, "My teacher gave this paper to me and told me to give it only to my mother."

As she read the letter, his mother's eyes became teary. But what she read aloud to her son was not the words on the page. Instead, she said aloud, as if reading the letter to her son, "Your son is a genius. This school is too small for him and doesn't have enough good teachers for training him. Please teach him yourself." So, she did.

Many years later, after Edison's mother died, he was recognized as one of the greatest inventors of the century. One day he was looking through old family things. Suddenly he saw a folded piece of paper in the back corner of a desk drawer. He took it and opened it. He recognized it as the childhood note he had brought home from school to his mother. On the paper it was written, "Your son is addled [mentally ill]. We won't let him come to school anymore."

Edison cried for hours. Then he wrote in his diary, "Thomas Alva Edison was an addled child that, by a hero mother, became the genius of the century."

Even young children can be inspired to aspire to do remarkable things. But they need role models. So, Brad Metzler, author of thriller historical novels and father of three, decided to provide some role models for his children. These stories became the start of his *Ordinary People Change the World* illustrated children's series, published by Dial. Each title begins with "I Am," for example, *I Am Albert Einstein*. Other titles in the series include the lives of the African-American baseball star Jackie Robinson; the chimpanzee researcher Jane Goodall; the television comedienne Lucille Ball; the civil-rights heroine Rosa Parks; the early aviator Amelia Earhart; and the Muppets chief puppeteer Jim Henson. In this book series, Brad Metzler tells how each of these people used their gifts and talents to put out messages of kindness, caring, daring, creativity, and goodness.

The success of God's project will require not only great inventors, scientists, researchers, astronauts, technicians, environmentalists, and powerful leaders, but also teachers, therapists, politicians, lawyers, doctors, dentists, nurses, businesspeople, journalists, managers, laborers, child-care workers, puppeteers and, above all, loving parents. Without all these people—like Leon collecting half-used rolls of toilet paper from office buildings and giving them to the poor—God's project could never move forward.

Every now and then, we hear inspiring stories of ordinary people whose unrecognized daily work has made an impact on human development. In 2016, a book by Margot Lee Shetterly titled *Hidden Figures* tells the story of a group of brilliant African American women who did classified mathematical work behind the scenes during the early days of the space program in NASA headquarters at Langley. This was after World War II and during the Cold War.[59] These women were human computers, geniuses with slide rules, crunching numbers and making by-hand calculations long before the digital age. They came up with the formulas and did the calculations themselves. For example, they were the ones that plotted the trajectory of John Glenn's historic flight that made him the first American to orbit the planet successfully.

Called the "West Computers," after the west area of Langley to which these black women were relegated and segregated, they helped blaze a trail for mathematicians and engineers of all races and genders to follow. These women provided the mathematical left cortex of NASA's brainpower. Their computing abilities accounted for many of NASA's advancements. Working diligently in their segregated area, they generated equations that described every function of a new plane or rocket, running the numbers often with no sense of the greater mission of the project. They also contributed to the ever-changing design of planes and rockets, making them faster, safer, and more aerodynamic.

Few of these women were acknowledged in academic publications or for their work on various projects. Not only were they rarely provided the same opportunities and titles as their male counterparts, but these "computers" of color were also forced to live with constant reminders that they were second-class citizens. Daily, they fought other seemingly small battles, against separate bathrooms and restricted access to meetings. It was these small battles and daily minutiae that Shetterly strove to capture in her book. Outside the workplace, they faced many more problems, including segregated buses and dilapidated schools for their children. Many struggled to find housing in Hampton, Virginia, the neighboring town. The white "computers" could live in Anne Wythe Hall, a dormitory at Langley that helped alleviate the shortage of housing. But the black "computers" were left to their own devices.

> "History is the sum total of what all of us do on a daily basis," said Shetterly. "We think of capital 'H' history as being these huge figures—George Washington, Alexander Hamilton

and Martin Luther King." Even so, she explains, "you go to
bed at night, you wake up the next morning, and then yes-
terday is history. These small actions in some ways are more
important or certainly as important as the individual actions
by these towering figures."[60]

Only in retrospect can we recognize the groundbreaking achieve-
ments of these "hidden figures." But to them, this was their job, their patri-
otic duty. Day after day, they did their work to the best of their ability.
They went to bed at night and woke up the next morning to go to work at
Langley, exercising the abilities God had given them for making history.
Veteran actress Sally Field is passionately involved in an organization called Vital Voices. It began in 2000, right after the Beijing Women's
Conference that was started by then Secretary of State Hillary Clinton.
Sally wrote, "I went away feeling that unless we could bring half
the world's population [women] to the table in important ways, the
world would never be really healthy—environmentally, economically,
politically."
The Vital Voices group "identifies and invests in emerging
women leaders, whether they're on a political level or leaders as far as
economics is concerned or human rights," says Field. Vital Voices goes
into small cities and communities to identify these emerging women
leaders who need to have their voices supported. Vital Voices "mentor
them and empower them to fulfill their dreams."[61]
Just as each of the variety of cells in your physical body must do
their specific jobs to keep you healthy and ever-maturing, so we learn
to think of ourselves as cells in the Christ Body, doing our particular
work, helping to keep the great Body healthy and ever-maturing. We
must play our parts in Christogenesis. Lovers want to do things for the
ones they love, and that includes doing things for the God we love and
for Christ's Body here on Earth, of which we are a part.
In India, there are more than a billion mobile phones in operation, even in some of the poorest households in rural areas. However,
the people of India speak an estimated 780 different languages and dialects. Unfortunately, just a few languages, like English and Hindi, have
been the only interfaces available on India's mobile phone system. So,
the poorest people who are not familiar with either English or Hindi
can only use their phones for basic calls. This was the case until a few
years ago.

Two college students, Umesh Sachdev and Ravi Saraogi, loved their home nation of India. They were inspired to create a software system called Uniphore that allows people to interact with their phones in their native languages. Their software includes a "virtual assistant" (like Siri on the iPhone) able to process more than 25 global languages and 150 dialects. Already, over five million people are using Uniphore's system. "Phones can help increase financial inclusion or help a farmer get weather information," says Sachdev, "but you need a way for people to interact with the technology out there."[62] These two college students have used resources—their knowledge of computer programming and language skills—to make a difference for thousands of people.

St. Catherine of Sienna said, "Be who God meant you to be and you will set the world on fire." Remember, most fires start with something as small as a match. In the physical world, a match may light a candle that dispels the darkness or a cigarette that harms a smoker's health. And a cigarette not completely extinguished and casually tossed aside can start a destructive forest fire. Symbolically, each of us is a like a small match. We can use that match to do something destructive or to bring new light into the world.

It is surprising that so many of the examples of people wanting to make a difference seem to be occurring among younger people. It's as if the young, more than any other age group, care about improving the world. Recent popes apparently realized this and began appealing to young people. During a prayer vigil before World Youth Day, Pope John Paul II said,

> It is Jesus who stirs in you the desire to do something great with your lives, the will to follow an ideal, the refusal to allow yourselves to be ground down by mediocrity, the courage to commit yourselves humbly and patiently to improving yourselves and society, making the world more human and more fraternal.[63]

Spiritual Exercise: What Kind of Match Are You?

Do you know of people who have lit a match to start an evolutionary fire? Who have used their abilities to make a positive—or negative—difference in the world? How have you been inspired to make a difference? Where did that inspiration come from?

ETHICAL PRINCIPLE 6:
Resources for the Evolutionary Process

———— Everyone has many resources for nurturing the evolutionary process. *(Derived from Basic Principles 2, 5, 6, 7, 8)*
    This ethical principle expands the previous principle that focused
on people using their love-energy resources *to nurture the evolutionary
process.* This ethical principle emphasizes identifying the number of
resources each one has and recognizing the many ways those resources
can be used.
———— Teilhard wants people to realize that they may have many more
resources than they believe they have. Unsuspected resources may
include one's time, talents, wealth, personality, knowledge, skills, life
experience, family, friendships, professional relationships, social position, influence, contacts and connections, level of consciousness, and
many other resources.
    Money is an obvious resource. In Kalamazoo, Michigan, several
anonymous donors have created Kalamazoo Promise with an $80 mil-
lion investment, so that any high school graduate from Kalamazoo that
wants to go to college can attend an in-state college for free. Since
2006, more than five thousand students have taken advantage of the
Promise. This generous educational venture has turned around the
fortunes of a city in the rust belt. Kalamazoo used to make Gibson
guitars and Checker cabs. The Promise also inspired President Barack
Obama to give his first high school commencement address at Kalamazoo Central High in 2010.[64]
    The Bill and Melinda Gates Foundation also supports college
scholarships worldwide. But these full scholarships may be most deeply
appreciated in the Native American community for students being
schooled on poor Indian reservations. In these reservation schools, eli-
gibility standards to win a "Gates" are exceptionally rigorous. In addition to maintaining a minimum GPA of 3.3 (out of 4.0), applicants
must demonstrate leadership skills and a commitment to community

service. Only one thousand scholars are selected each year from a pool of over thirty-five thousand applicants. For those who earn the scholarship, it represents an extraordinary opportunity to pursue both personal and professional dreams.

I regularly receive a newsletter from the Red Cloud Indian School in Pine Ridge, South Dakota. A recent newsletter included a photo of five happy seniors who received Gates scholarships.[65] Also this year, the Red Cloud Middle School introduced courses in computer programming and robotics, hoping to use them to gain more scholarships in future years.

In addition to the scholarship providers, there are literally tens of thousands of ordinary people who donate money regularly to schools on Indian reservations, so that these schools may continue to operate.

But money isn't the only resource — or the most powerful. Among talents that people have but don't often think of as resources include leadership, humor, mothering qualities, storytelling, calming people down, investing money, finding alternatives, creativity, organization, reconciling, picking up after others, cooking, coming up with slogans, a gift for selling things.

People enter careers and professions for many reasons: money, status, security. But some people have experiences that turn a career into a greater sense of purpose. These experiences energize the self in new and unexpected ways. Such people still live up to the standard of excellence inherent in their field, but something special gets added — an open concern for people beyond themselves.

At the start of the twentieth century, a young New York socialite, Frances Perkins, became an activist for progressive causes. She was a polite young woman with a rather refined personality. On March 25, 1911, she happened to be in Greenwich Village in Manhattan near the scene when the Triangle Shirtwaist factory burned.

It was the deadliest industrial disaster in the history of the city, and one of the deadliest in the history of the United States. The fire caused the deaths of 146 garment workers — 123 women and 23 men. They died from fire, smoke inhalation, or falling or jumping to their deaths. Most of the victims were recent Jewish and Italian immigrant women aged sixteen to twenty-three.

Francis watched dozens of garment workers from the ninth and tenth floors hurl themselves to their deaths rather than be burned alive. That experience awakened her moral and ethical sensibilities, expanded her consciousness of working conditions for the poor, and refocused her personal ambition. It was a moral crisis moment for her.

"After that, she turned herself into an instrument for the cause of workers' rights. She was willing to work with anybody, compromise with anybody, push through hesitation." She even changed her "upper class" appearance by wearing more ordinary clothes, so she could become a more effective instrument for the movement. During Franklin D. Roosevelt's presidency, she became the first woman in the president's cabinet. She emerged as one of the great civic figures of the twentieth century.[66]

Two well-known psychiatrists, T. Berry Brazelton, MD, and Stanley I. Greenspan, MD, reinforce Teilhard's ethical principle about the untapped potential of people.

The potential of human beings is enormous. All children come into life with a wide variety of inborn, biosocial systems that favor the actualization of their potential.

Yet, for millions of years, humans have not had much accurate information for actualizing that potential. Most children were taught how to interact based on the experience or inexperience of their parents. Much of the commonly held folklore about socialization is incorrect and detrimental to full development. Today, we have a great deal of useful information that can help people learn how easy it can be to nurture children's potential wisely.

We now know that this potential is virtually untapped, containing the possibilities for doing both creative and positive behavior as well as destructive and negative behavior. We are learning how to help parents and teachers develop the creative aspects of the children in their charge, helping them learn to do things that make the world a better place for themselves and others, discovering the countless ways that people in relationships and teams can develop their own unique abilities in rewarding and positive ways.[67]

Even search engines like Google and Yahoo are resources easily available to everyone. On them you can find the information that you need, and you can do it in moments. How to find a certain neurosurgeon? How to find a specific brand and model of an athletic shoe? How to find your genealogical roots? How to find a marriageable mate? How to find your favorite Scripture quote in its original Greek script?

Other resources include people you know who can do something that you can't, or they have a connection to someone who can.

In 2012, a technique for editing a genetic code was invented called CRISPR-Cas9, opening one of the most expansive frontiers ever contemplated by science. It was led by two biological research groups who shared a mutual goal. They teamed up, using their respective expertise and resources, to figure out the process of gene editing to develop an actual tool that could do it. One group was led by Jennifer Doudna from the University of California at Berkeley, who is an expert in RNA. The other group, working half a world away, was led by Emmanuelle Charpentier, then at Umea University in Sweden and now at the Max Planck Institute in Germany. By sharing their research with each other, they discovered that an enzyme in the cells—named Cas9—could function as a powerful pair of molecular scissors.

Four years later, CRISPR-Cas9 is producing helpful results in every area of biology. Today, you can go online to many biology supply companies and buy your own CRISPR kit for about $130. The technique is being used in hundreds of labs across the world.[68]

Here is the revolutionary power of this "molecular scissors" technique: in the past, to figure out what effect a specific gene had on a certain type of cancer tumor, you had to breed mice without that gene and with that tumor to see what effect it had on the cancer. Such research might take many months and yield no positive results, explained cancer biologist Scott Lowe at Memorial Sloan Cancer Center in New York. "Now CRISPR makes it very easy in an afternoon to knock out a gene and study what effect it has on the tumor," Lowe says.[69]

While some resources may live an ocean away, sometimes the resource you need may be sitting in the car behind you.

Daily commuters driving to work in slow traffic can't compare their distress to the daily ordeal faced by millions of parents of school-age children: *the afternoon dismissal car waiting line.* Some parents get in line forty-five minutes before dismissal and wait to get a good spot and avoid an additional half-hour in gridlock.

A Tampa dad, Pat Bhava, the father of a fifth grader, found himself sitting in a car line every day enduring a thirty- to forty-five-minute wait for his son's classes to end. He decided to do something about it. He and another waiting dad, who understood advanced algorithms and relational positioning methodology, created a PikMyKid app to streamline the process of picking up kids after school.[70]

You may be surprised by the many loving resources you have besides the talents and skills you learned at school. You probably never thought of them as your resources. Certain personal qualities that are powerful loving resources include honesty, determination, optimism, unflappability, patience, humor, reconciliation, and so forth. At unsuspecting moments, a single action with your special talent can make a difference.

Sandy was a very popular girl at school. One day, she had a chance to use that popularity resource to help a shy student, MaryLou, who was being bullied. Sandy saw this group of girls circled around MaryLou, teasing and taunting her. Instead of telling the group to stop bullying, Sandy merely walked through the group, right up to MaryLou. The group hushed, expecting Sandy would join in the taunting. Instead, she took MaryLou by the hand, and loudly said, "How about you and I have lunch together today? I would like to be your friend." From that day forward, no one ever bullied MaryLou.

Jackson had a knack for algebra. It came easy to him. He noticed that Tyler was having difficulty solving equations. Instead of thinking that Tyler's problems with algebra were Tyler's and not his, Jackson suggested that he and Tyler might become study partners. Jackson realized he would be giving up some of his free time, but he also realized that Tyler was genuinely trying to succeed, and Jackson felt the desire to help him. They did become study partners, but they also became friends and found a summer job at a camp where they both worked together. It turned out that Tyler was a natural counselor and knew how to deal with the kids in camp, while Jackson was having trouble relating to the young campers. This time, Tyler became Jackson's tutor.

Devon Kemp, a young woman studying at the Boston College School of Theology and Ministry, said, "I've spent much of my life in faith formation of young people, both at the parish and the university. It is clear to me that the Holy Spirit is alive among the young, touching their hearts and stretching them to service of others. There is something deep and true in our world today: the coexistence of fear and hope among the young, and the desire to bring forth love as a path toward a better world."[71]

Spiritual Exercise: List Your Resources

Start by listing your skills and talents, what you have learned and been trained to do. Then add to that list some of your personal qualities, such as leadership, popularity, honesty, optimism, patience, sense of humor, and faith. Then note the places and situations where you can use your many resources.

ETHICAL PRINCIPLE 7:
Ethical Obligations May Change over Time

One's ethical obligations may change over time, depending on one's change in available resources or level of spiritual growth. *(Derived from Basic Principles 1, 2, 3, 4)*

Traditionally, everyone, no matter their social status, had the same moral challenge. As Ignatius put it in the beginning of the *Spiritual Exercises*, "You were created to praise, reverence and serve God Our Lord and by this means to save your soul."[72] In that traditional world perspective, it didn't matter whether you were rich or poor, gifted or developmentally challenged, sick or healthy. Your single moral obligation was to save your soul.

By contrast, in the world of God's project, your primary moral obligation is to help build the Body of Christ. That's how you show your praise, reverence, gratitude, and love for God. In an evolving world, that is your new moral obligation—to help build the Body of Christ. There are no clear rules on how to do it. Your contribution is up to you to discover.

In his Letter to the Romans, Paul points out that we all have our special work cut out for us in helping build the kingdom of God (see Rom 12:4–21). Each of us has work that is uniquely ours in helping complete God's project. These are the positive contributions each of us is, as it were, "assigned by God" to accomplish.

> For as in one body we have many members, and not all the members have the same function, so we, who are many, are one body in Christ, and individually we are members one of another. We have gifts that differ according to the grace given to us: prophecy, in proportion to faith; ministry, in ministering; the teacher, in teaching; the exhorter, in exhortation; the giver, in generosity; the leader, in diligence; the compassionate, in cheerfulness. (Rom 12:4–8)

Paul lists some obvious roles that are needed to preserve the life and growth of the believing community in the early church: prophecy, teaching, exhorting, donating time and money, leadership, showing compassion, and, most interestingly, those whose task it is to bring joy and hope to the community.

Paul's sense of "evolution" was to extend the good news all over the towns and villages of Asia and Europe. His secret for spreading the good news of God's unconditional love for all people was to get all his new Christian converts to live "according to the Spirit." He described what it meant to live in the Spirit. The following list of spiritual tactics made up Paul's paradoxical strategy to transform the world:

> Rejoice in hope, be patient in suffering, persevere in prayer. Contribute to the needs of the saints; extend hospitality to strangers. Bless those who persecute you; bless and do not curse them. Rejoice with those who rejoice, weep with those who weep. Live in harmony with one another; do not be haughty, but associate with the lowly; do not claim to be wiser than you are. Do not repay anyone evil for evil, but take thought for what is noble in the sight of all. If it is possible, so far as it depends on you, live peaceably with all. Beloved, never avenge yourselves....No, "if your enemies are hungry, feed them; if they are thirsty, give them something to drink; for by doing this you will heap burning coals on their heads." Do not be overcome by evil, but overcome evil with good. (Rom 12:12–21)

Paul believed the good news would eventually reach everywhere simply by the continuous flow of this merciful and loving behavior. Others would see the joy and compassion of these Christians, be touched by it, and inquire where it came from. As they learned of the good news of God's love, they, too, would come to welcome it and be transformed by it. It was Paul's vision that, eventually, the loving behavior of Christians would transform the world.

Teilhard's evolutionary vision contains many elements of Paul's vision. It would certainly include getting everyone to live according to the Spirit, which ethically requires far more than simply avoiding sin.

In addition to the unique roles assigned by God that Paul listed in Romans 12:4–8, Teilhard would add some others: developing teams for research, scientific exploration, technological creativity, dealing with world health problems such as poverty and disease, and caring for the Earth and the environment.[73] Teilhard found support for this in Paul's writing, for Paul clearly recognized that even nature itself, going through labor pains, is undergoing an evolutionary process that has not yet been fulfilled:

> For the creation waits with eager longing…in hope that the creation itself will be set free from its bondage to decay and will obtain the freedom of the glory of the children of God. We know that the whole creation has been groaning in labor pains until now. (Rom 8:19–22)

Spiritual Exercise: No Clear Rules

Can you name some areas of life where you feel an urge to make a difference, yet you can find no clear moral rules on how to make a positive contribution? Perhaps you would like to help improve working conditions for women, or get involved in caring for the environment, or want to help ease racial tensions or combat certain social prejudices in your neighborhood.

A Developmental Morality and Ethic

This seventh ethical principle also emphasizes that one's obligations to be of service to God's project may change over time, or that present forms of service may be enriched simply as one matures morally. For Teilhard, evolutionary ethics calls essentially for a developmental morality. "From everyone to whom much has been given, much will be required" (Luke 12:48).

Frances Perkins, who witnessed the Triangle Shirtwaist factory fire in 1911, went through several stages of moral growth. Recall that she grew up as a young socialite from a wealthy family, enjoying many privileges in New York society. She had her first moment of moral growth when she realized there were many important progressive causes that needed support and advocated for them. The second moment of inner change, noted earlier, happened when she witnessed the great fire and realized the unsafe conditions in which poorer laborers worked. She had a third stage of growth when she realized that such workers would not trust a woman wearing elegant clothing. So, she learned to dress in ways that did not make them suspicious of her sincerity. She had another stage of moral development when she began to work for the government in President Roosevelt's cabinet. To achieve some of her goals for workers, she had to learn to bargain, to cooperate, to concede, and to adapt to political party pressures at the national level. As she matured in her moral consciousness, she was challenged repeatedly to enrich her mindset and her way of interacting if she hoped to invest her talents to make a positive difference in a very complex and competitive world.

Jesus suggested this same ethical principle in his story about the man who went off and entrusted his stewards with money (see Matt 25:14–30). To one he gave ten talents, to another five, and to a third one. (You may think of a "talent" as a measure of money, probably about a million dollars in today's currency.) The steward with ten talents doubled his master's investment in him, as did the one given five talents. The third servant merely hid his talent and gave it back to the master on his return. Notice that in Jesus's story, the third servant was labeled a "worthless servant."

One's ethical responsibilities may also increase in proportion to one's moral development as well as to one's "resources" (as enumerated earlier). For example, as people grow and develop in their careers and enjoy more potential to influence things, their ethical responsibilities may increase and at times come into conflict with the ethical beliefs of others and even with the church.

When Dr. Gregory Pincus, inventor of the "Pill," asked Dr. John Rock (1890–1984) to collaborate with him on clinical trials for an oral contraceptive, Rock seemed an unlikely choice. This highly regarded obstetrician and gynecologist was a devout Roman Catholic. However, he was also a groundbreaking infertility specialist, who devoted much of his career to helping women with fertility problems to conceive.

Throughout his practice, Rock had witnessed the suffering that women endured from unwanted pregnancies. He had seen collapsed wombs, premature aging, and desperation caused by too many mouths to feed. These challenging experiences of his patients had a profound impact on the doctor. Despite his faithful Catholicism and the church's opposition to contraceptives, Rock came to support contraception within the confines of marriage. He believed in the power of birth control to stem poverty and prevent medical problems associated with pregnancy.

Although Rock had a progressive view of birth control, he was a social conservative. A father of five and grandfather of fourteen, he attended Mass daily and kept a crucifix on the wall above his office desk.

When Rock was a young boy, his parish priest had taken him aside and admonished him, "John, always stick to your conscience. Never let anyone keep it for you." According to Rock, these words of advice were to become his life's guiding principle.

As a professor of obstetrics and gynecology at Harvard Medical School in the 1940s, Dr. Rock taught his students about birth control, something unheard of in medical schools at the time. In 1949, he coauthored a book, *Voluntary Parenthood*, explaining birth control methods for the general reader. By the time Gregory Pincus approached Rock in the early 1950s about helping with trials for the Pill, Rock had also come to believe in the need for world population control.

At a time in his life when he could have been settling into comfortable retirement, Rock agreed to work with Pincus on the controversial project to create a "magic pill" contraceptive. As part of the infertility research at his clinic, Rock was able to conduct the first human trials for the Pill in Boston and sidestep Massachusetts's rigid anti-birth control law.

When the Pill received FDA approval in 1960, Rock's work on behalf of the Pill came to the forefront. At age 70, Rock launched a one-man campaign to gain Vatican approval of the Pill. Rock argued that using the Pill was a more precise way of following the rhythm method. He strongly believed that the church should consider it a "natural," and therefore acceptable form of birth control, because it contained the same hormones already present in every woman's reproductive system and just extended the "safe period" a woman would have every month.

In 1963, Rock gained national attention for his cause with the publication of *The Time Has Come: A Catholic Doctor's Proposals to End the Battle over Birth Control*. The debate sparked by Rock's book received wide publicity, and he was featured in *Time* magazine, on the cover of *Newsweek*, and on a one-hour NBC television program. As Rock became a familiar figure in America and abroad, his view quickly took root among the laity of the church as well as among many Catholic religious leaders.

Rock was crushed when, in 1968, the pope officially banned the Pill in the encyclical *Humanae Vitae* (On Human Life).

Yet, despite the church's continued opposition to the Pill, a profound change had taken place among Catholic believers. Since the encyclical, millions of Catholics around the world have chosen to follow their own consciences on the matter of birth control. Rock's views on the Pill, once daring and radical, have become commonplace among the rank and file of church congregations. Although he died feeling that he had failed in his mission, John Rock's contribution to the debate on birth control had a profound impact not only on the lives of countless Catholic women but also on women of all races and religions all over the world.

Spiritual Exercise:
Welcoming Growth and Development

The story about the three stewards entrusted with talents given to them by their master may be interpreted as a metaphor for the talents God (our master) has given to each of us to help achieve God's project. Do you identify with any of the three stewards? How are you like them or different from them? How have you "invested" your talents?

The Process of Moral Development

One significant way to develop your ability to foster God's project is to develop yourself. Teilhard called this process *self-evolution*.[74] David Brooks wrote an article for the *New York Times* that exemplifies this sense of moral development or self-evolution.

> About once a month, I run across a person who radiates an inner light. These people can be in any walk of life. They seem deeply good. They listen well. They make you feel valued. You often catch them looking after other people and, as they do so, their laugh is musical, and their manner is infused with gratitude. They are not thinking about what wonderful work they are doing. They are not thinking about themselves at all.

When I meet such a person, it brightens my entire day. But I confess that I often have a sadder thought: It occurs to me that I've achieved a decent level of career success, but I have not achieved that inner light. I have not achieved that generosity of spirit, or that depth of character.

A few years ago, I realized that I wanted to be more like those people. I realized that to achieve this I was going to have to work harder to save my own soul. I was going to have to have the sort of moral adventures that produce that kind of goodness. I was going to have to be better at balancing my life.

It occurred to me that there were two sets of virtues, the résumé virtues and the eulogy virtues. The résumé virtues are the skills you bring to the marketplace. The eulogy virtues are the ones that are talked about at your funeral — whether you were kind, brave, honest, or faithful. Were you capable of deep love?

So, a few years ago, I set out to discover how those deeply good people got that way. I didn't know if I could follow their road to character (I'm a pundit, paid to appear smarter and better than I really am). But I wanted to know what the road looked like.

I concluded that wonderful people are made, not born — that the people I admired had achieved an unfakeable inner virtue, built slowly from specific moral and spiritual accomplishments.

If we want to be gimmicky, we could say these accomplishments amounted to a moral bucket list, the experiences one should have on the way toward the richest possible inner life.[75]

Brooks went on to develop his own moral bucket list. Some of the items included humility, taming his personal weaknesses, accepting "redemptive" assistance from others, developing energizing love, decentering himself, recognizing the inner call within his calling, and developing a character with a conscience.

He ended his long essay with this powerful contrast:

Commencement speakers are always telling young people to follow their passions. Be true to yourself. This is a vision of life that begins with self and ends with self. But people on the road to inner light do not find their vocations by asking, what do I want from life? They ask, what is life asking of me? How can I match my intrinsic talent with one of the world's deep needs?

Spiritual Exercise: Changing Ethical Obligations

It is obvious that David Brooks's level of spiritual growth had changed over the years, since it is not likely that when he graduated college his list of accomplishments was not those of his spiritual bucket list. How has your spiritual bucket list changed over the years? Are you still seeking those things you sought when you were in your teens and twenties?

ETHICAL PRINCIPLE 8: Sins of Omission

In an evolutionary ethic, the primary personal sins are sins of omission. (*Derived from Basic Principles 2, 3, 7, 8*)

Teilhard's Basic Form of Sin

Teilhard's thoughts on sin are not easy to find in his writings. According to Robert Faricy, people will look in vain among Teilhard's essays and papers for any consideration of sin in *the way most people think of sin*—as a personal psychological choice, or as a subjective existential act, or as a personal and subjective rejection of God's love.[76]

So, where does Teilhard look for sin? The theological questions that interested him were those that touched upon the question of the evolution of the universe toward our fulfillment in Christ.[77] For him, *the most important sins are those that most delay and hinder the forward and upward progress of the Body of Christ.* He is most concerned about whatever could block the full accomplishment of God's project.

When Teilhard talks about sin, he looks at it in a much larger context. It is almost always in the context of all the unavoidable evils

120

and diminishments happening in creation in general—conflict, confusion, competition, fear, loss, suffering, grief, and so on. These are the often-destructive experiences that must be endured in the forward movement of creation, the diminishments that inevitably accompany the evolutionary process. For him, traditional sins of commission form only a small part of all these evils or diminishments that have been happening since the start of the universe and continue even today.

Teilhard does not equate evil with sin. For him, the name *sin* may be applied *only to those evils consciously generated by creatures that have evolved to self-reflective consciousness, namely, mature human persons.* He sees evil as a much broader category.

Animals and nature can also cause evil or diminishment in the world around them. Hungry deer can eat much of your garden. A frustrated dog may chew your bedroom slippers to shreds. Termites can ruin your home. Mold and mildew can make your house unlivable. A tornado may blow the roof off your barn. A flood can destroy your business. Such evil is inevitable because of the multiplicity of events on the planet and the current impossibility of every animal and every part of nature to survive. Nature is not yet mature enough for all creatures to act together in loving union. Creation is not yet at the stage where the lion lies down with the lamb. At this stage, today, the lion still attacks and kills the lamb, then eats it.

Teilhard reminds us that almost all the evils and unwelcome events, like death and destruction that happen around us, are statistically inevitable. It is so because the complex multiplicity of the elements of the universe are still fumbling forward in their evolutionary process of cosmogenesis. The universe is still trying to grow toward its maturity through its cosmic gestation processes. Teilhard constantly reminds us that we are still amid an evolutionary process, and evil will remain an inevitable part of that process until the process reaches its completion.

Humans often cause evil or diminishment to themselves, others, and nature simply because of the confusion, congestion, and complexity of the human family. There are billions of us moving around the planet, and all of us have multiple agendas we want to accomplish. However, many of our plans and desires conflict with those of others. This causes suffering. As individuals and nations, we still wage war and harm each another to achieve our objectives. We are in a process that Teilhard calls *anthropogenesis*, the process of maturation of humanity. Because of the multiplicity and complexity of human relationships in this evolutionary process, consciously produced human evil—including sin—is inevitable.

For example, suppose there is a job opening for which one hundred people apply. In the end, one applicant is chosen while the other ninety-nine are rejected. For the one person chosen for the job, the event was a *beneficial gift*. For the other ninety-nine, the event was an unwelcome *diminishment*. That's a ninety-nine-to-one ratio of diminishment.

Among the ninety-nine, many will generate some form of "evil." Some will feel angry and vent that anger outwardly, perhaps on members of their family. Others will feel discarded and resentful and may turn to violence. Still others will become discouraged or depressed and blame themselves. Still others will become anxious and maybe do something they will regret later. Maybe one of the rejected will commit suicide.

Many of these various responses may not qualify as truly free choices—or sins—but the pain and suffering that flow from those, perhaps impulsive, actions are inevitable—and are very real. Perhaps, one of the ninety-nine will become a drug dealer and help generate dozens of addicts. Or the person who commits suicide leaves behind a deeply grieving family and children who will be shunned at school as the children of a suicide.

Moreover, repercussions from each of the actions and reactions of the ninety-nine may leave long-term traces on the world. Many a terrorist has been known to have been rejected by family, or thrown out of school, or unable to qualify for a desirable job.

For Teilhard, personal choices and actions that produce evil and diminishment are, for the most part, inevitable and unavoidable. Because they are inevitable and unavoidable, they are forgivable by God who is lovingly and patiently involved observing our evolutionary process.

Teilhard has been accused of using abstract and impersonal terms to describe sin. For example, he sometimes defines *sin* as "a return to multiplicity" or "a movement away from unity and organization." He uses terms like these because, for him, the goal of God's project is to bring about a loving unity of all creation. Anything that detracts from that ultimate unity is evil. *When an action that harms or destroys some loving unity is carried out with reflective consciousness and free consent, Teilhard would label that act a "sin."*

For example, a good marriage is a loving unity and certainly a part of God's plan. To break up that marriage is to "return [a loving unity] to multiplicity." Similarly, suppose there is a well-organized team of researchers working on a new vaccine. If someone were determined to create animosity among team members and, in turn, defeat the success of their research, it would be an attempt to produce a "movement away from unity and organization." For Teilhard, everything is measured as good or evil in terms of its effect on the goal of God's plan. Does it promote or hinder the growth of our loving union in the Body of Christ?

Teilhard would describe *sin* as any deliberate movement of human free choice away from unity. Teilhard says it boldly: "There is *only one evil*: disunity. We call it 'moral' when it affects the free zones of the soul."[78]

Teilhard is not focused on our human weaknesses or on our failures due to those weaknesses. Nor is he primarily concerned with the ordinary "sins" we so often confess in the sacrament of reconciliation, like impatience, bad thoughts, arguments, petty lies. He is focused on sins that consciously promote disunity. He especially notes those actions we could easily have performed, but didn't, that would have nurtured in some little way a sense of unity in a marriage, a friendship, a team, or even a nation. These loving unions are the building blocks of the Body of Christ. To refuse to support them is to harm God's project.

Teilhard wants to reverse the traditional emphasis focused on personal sin and forgiveness. For example, he says we need "a baptism in which purification [from sin] becomes a subordinate element in the total divine act of raising the world." We also need "a cross which symbolizes much more the ascent of creation through effort than the expiations of an offense."[79]

Teilhard is always focused on God's project. For him, any analysis of morality and ethics must stem from that consideration. He is writing specifically to those who are committed to building the Body of Christ. From this forward-looking and active perspective, Teilhard focuses on two areas that are most important for these positive builders to be aware of: *sins of omission* and *social sins*.

Spiritual Exercise: Sin and God's Project

Recall Teilhard's first ethical principle: ethics is about guiding human choices and behavior in such a way that they make a positive difference in helping promote and advance God's evolutionary project. *This is always Teilhard's focus. He wants us always to be conscious of it as we think about personal and collective sin. Is it becoming your focus?*

Sins of Omission

—— Traditionally, the most important sins were sins of commission—violations of the Ten Commandments. Concern for sins of omission wasn't even recognized in the church's official liturgical prayer until the revisions of the Mass text after Vatican II. Liturgists added eight very crucial words to the *Confetior* prayer at the beginning of mass. "I confess to almighty God and to you, my brothers and sisters, that I have greatly sinned in my thoughts and words, in what I have done *and in what I have failed to do.*" For the first time in hundreds of years came the public acknowledgment that sins of omission were important.

For Teilhard, the potential good that sins of omission leave undone may be crucial. In terms of accomplishing God's project, sins of omission may be more important than sins of commission because work on the divine project that you or I could have done is left undone.

For example, if your goal is to build a new home for your family, examples of sins of *commission*, on the one hand, might be workers stealing some lumber to take home for themselves or lazily doing some faulty work that has to be redone. On the other hand, sins of *omission* might include workers not coming to work at all, or the superintendent not bothering to give directions to the workers, or the architect never clearly drawing up detailed plans for the building. These sins of omission are more important because the necessary construction work never gets done, and your new home never gets built properly. Think of God's project for the world—and imagine that nobody shows up for work. That's a metaphor for sins of omission.

For Teilhard, such sins of omission are crucial. If there is something that offers hope of furthering God's project that I alone can do here and now, and I don't do it, *it doesn't get done.* This principle applies even to simple acts of human kindness. For example, if I see clearly that someone needs a smile, an encouraging word or a helpful hand, and I consciously refuse to respond, that kindness doesn't get done. For Teilhard, the refusal to perform some good work in cooperation with God's evolutionary grace qualifies as a sin. This is Jesus's message in the parable of the Good Samaritan. It is why he begins the story with the "sins of omission" committed by the priest and Levite who saw an opportunity to show compassion, but simply kept walking.

For Teilhard, from this "omission" perspective, some of the worst sins are those by people who, besides doing nothing, belittle or hinder workers who were planning to go to work on God's project. These naysayers would hold back those who were planning to do things to improve the life of the human family and the Earth. Among Teilhard's list of such sins of omission, they would be committed by

- *Critics*, who, instead of supporting workers who are trying to make a better world, prefer to put them down.
- *Bystanders*, who could just as easily join in the good work, but simply watch in quiet amusement—and might even prefer to see the work fail.
- *Cynics*, who not only refuse to believe that anything can be changed for the better, but who also try to spread their negativity.
- *Complainers*, who, instead of adding their effort for the success of a project, would rather complain than help.
- *Verbal Abusers*, who use their clever minds to deride, ridicule, and otherwise malign the people who are trying to do good.
- *Excusers*, who are always too busy to help, who refuse to get involved, or who want to do nothing.

We easily recognize each of these kinds of people in our own lives. Some of us may even find ourselves at times slipping easily into one or other of these categories.

Teilhard finds the behavior of critics, bystanders, pessimists, and the rest doubly evil. Not only do they not do any work personally to help God's cause, but by their words and example, they also encourage *others* not to contribute or to abandon the project. They create more activities of omission beyond their own.

Albert Einstein had even harsher words for such bystanders. He said, "The world will not be destroyed by those who do evil, but by those who watch them without doing anything."

What you may notice about these groups is that their words and actions are, in Teilhard's language, *activities of diminishment*. These are conscious choices that negatively affect themselves and others as well as God's project.

Still, Teilhard would acknowledge that all these categories of negative people and their evil effects are inevitable. They are unavoidable in a world where spiritual immaturity is still the norm. They are inescapable on a crowded planet that is still in the slow process of unifying itself in love.[80] Teilhard regards the negative behavior of such people, for the most part, as forgivable by God precisely because their actions don't qualify as truly sinful. In these activities of diminishment, most of the perpetrators are not operating fully in what Teilhard calls "the free zones of the soul." One is reminded of Jesus's first words on the cross: "Father, forgive them; for they do not know what they are doing" (Luke 23:34).

Some of these negative attitudes and patterns of behaviors among the critics, bystanders, and the rest may have been learned during childhood by copying what they saw others doing. Perhaps their parents or older siblings consistently modeled one or more of these negative attitudes. So as grown-ups, they are merely unconsciously repeating the immature behavioral habits of their parents. Only when they become conscious of these unhelpful and irresponsible attitudes and behaviors—and continue to do them—can they be called morally sinful.

Although the choices of cynics, critics, and bystanders are understandable, inevitable, and forgivable, the effects of their actions are still very real. Things that could have been done for Christ never got done.

Spiritual Exercise:
Critics, Complainers, and Bystanders.

Do you sometimes qualify as one of these naysayers on the list above? Do you know of anyone who is a chronic critic of people who are trying to do something good and worthwhile?

Teilhard's Examination of Conscience

In examining our conscience each day, Teilhard would have us ask ourselves questions at two levels.

In the short run:

- "What have I done for Christ (or God's project) today?"
- "What could I have done that I did not do?"
- "What can I do for Christ (or God's project) tomorrow?"

In the longer run:

- "What is the greater work that God is calling me to contribute to the divine project in Christ?"
- "What is my life's work for God's project? Am I preparing for it? Am I working on it? How is it progressing?"

The *short-run questions,* of course, may refer to elements or stages in the long-run questions. For instance, if I am writing a book, I may ask, "What have I produced toward my book today?" "What do I plan to accomplish on it tomorrow?" But mostly, the short-run questions refer to my behavior in general among the people I have interacted with today. "Did I treat family members with compassion, understanding, patience, forgiveness, and so on?" "At work, what could I have done to show that I was more understanding of a co-worker?" "Did I miss an opportunity to affirm my children today?" "Did I express gratitude to my spouse today?"

The *longer-run questions* have more to do with long-term goals or objectives. What can I do with my life this year that would help move God's project forward? What talents or resources am I using in my larger contributions to God's work? How can I use these resources better? How can I reorient my work so that it is more likely to succeed and contribute to the betterment of the planet?

Teilhard certainly saw his contribution to God's project clearly. He might have formulated it by saying that his destiny on Earth was *to show how the knowledge we have from science and evolution is not in contradiction to Christian beliefs but can enrich those beliefs.* He was deeply convinced that this was the work he was called to do by God. It was his mission.

What he discovered to his dismay was that his ideas were found unacceptable by church censors in Rome. Still, he remained true to his discerned mission as a priest and Jesuit. He kept writing. He tried enlisting his supportive contacts in the Society of Jesus and the church to intercede for him at the Vatican. He expressed his willingness to edit and revise his manuscripts in hopes of making clearer the connection between his thought, Scripture, and the doctrines of the church.

127

Unfortunately, none of these attempts succeeded. He was ordered not to speak of his theological ideas in public.

Despite the multiple rejections and diminishments that he endured from his Jesuit superiors and from Rome, he felt at peace as he continued his exploration of these topics. He hoped and trusted that, one day, his writings would see the light of day and be published.

Another major part of Teilhard's life mission was working as a scientist. His religious order and the church had no problem with his work in the scientific sphere. Throughout his life, he continued to make research contributions to the fields of geology and paleo-anthropology. He is credited with over 1,500 published scientific papers in these fields.

Spiritual Exercise: Questions for Reflection

Consider the long-run and short-run question posed above. Have you tried exploring each of these questions as they might apply to you personally? Do you know anyone who is aware of his or her life purpose and is following it?

The Holy Spirit at Work

The Holy Spirit gives us the power to love *a bit more powerfully than we could before*. The Holy Spirit enables us to make a difference in our families and communities. The Holy Spirit is always inspiring us to *do something more*, to go beyond the "normal," the "customary," the "expected."

A very simple example is offered by a little girl who walked to school every day. Like others, she often noticed the litter of paper, cups, cans, and bags that others had thoughtlessly dropped along the sidewalk during the previous evening. Except, this little girl was inspired by the Holy Spirit to do something more. She had a change of heart. So, each morning on her walk to school, she would take a plastic bag and pick up the things people had mindlessly dropped along the sidewalk. She would put them in the bag and drop the bag in the recycling bin at school. She would then carefully wash her hands and go to class. She was inspired to make her world look a little nicer. That is the way the Holy Spirit works within minds and hearts.

There was a wonderful change-of-heart story in a local Tampa Bay newspaper about a policeman, Bruce Roberts, and his relationship to the homeless. Part of the officer's job was to deal with the people who lived on the streets. In most cases, he would rouse homeless people sleeping on benches to get up and move along or, if necessary, arrest them for vagrancy. In his ordinary law enforcement mindset, homeless people were an annoyance to the community. In his way of seeing things, however, he developed what Teilhard would call "new eyes." He began to picture these men (most of them were men) as "orphans of the community" rather than as "annoyances to the community." So, he began asking them if they were receiving Social Security checks each month to live on. Many had no idea that they might be entitled to society's help.

Since his job as a patrolman was not to drive a homeless person in his police car to a Social Security office, he enlisted the help of a sheriff's deputy, Stephanie Krager. When the officer brought the first homeless man in, she drove him to the local Social Security office and accompanied him inside. She sat down with him at the agent's desk and helped with the paperwork. "The homeless need a hand," Krager said. "They don't know how to navigate the system."

In some cases, Krager could reach an arrangement so that the homeless person would get enough money monthly to afford a low-cost rental unit and have a home. At first, this "homeless initiative" started as a one-deputy operation. Today, six years later in St. Petersburg, Florida, there is a Homeless Initiative office, where homeless persons can get help to fill out paperwork and meet with other service providers.

"Our goal is to work with the chronically homeless, the most difficult cases," Krager said, "the mentally ill, the substance abusers, the ones who have been on the streets for 15, 20 years, and get them permanent supportive housing."

So far, her office team has helped more than five hundred homeless people find temporary housing or shelter. They have helped two hundred others find permanent housing, including those they've reunited with family.[81]

Spiritual Exercise: A New Perspective

Have you ever had an experience that changed your perception of an individual or a certain group of people, as the police officer did when he saw the homeless as "orphans of the community" rather than as "annoyances to the community"?

New Perspectives

In his letters to early Christians, Paul highlights some daily moral and ethical challenges. He enumerates actions all of us are called to do in bringing about the kingdom of God. No one is excused from them.[82]

Jesus also emphasized a change of heart in his followers. In his Sermon on the Mount, Jesus says he has come to show us a higher way, a more transcending mindset, that befits his followers whose role in life is to be "the salt of the earth" and "the light of the world" (Matt 5:13, 14; see also v. 17). Here are a few examples of a mindset shift from a traditional Stage One to a higher Stage Two from Jesus's perspective.

The old covenant said, "You shall not murder"; and "Whoever murders shall be liable to judgment" (Stage One). "But I say to you that if you are angry with a brother or sister, you will be liable to judgment" (Stage Two).

The old covenant said, "You shall not commit adultery" (Stage One). "But I say to you that everyone who looks at a woman with lust has already committed adultery with her in his heart" (Stage Two).

The old covenant said if you were harmed, you could retaliate equally: "An eye for an eye and a tooth for a tooth" (Stage One). Jesus says not to retaliate at all (Stage Two).

The old covenant said to love your neighbor but hate your enemy (Stage One). Jesus says to love your enemy (Stage Two) (see Matt 7:21–45).

This is the essence of Jesus's new perspective, finding a higher way of living, using a more all-inclusive consciousness.

Spiritual Exercise: A New Life Purpose

How have you experienced the two stages of response in your life? Do you know of someone who has manifested the second stages of response in their life?

ETHICAL PRINCIPLE 9:
Social Sin[83]

Confronting social sin is especially important in an evolutionary world. *(Derived from Basic Principles 1, 2, 3, 4, 7)*

Sins that have become fixtures in the social structure are among the most difficult to eradicate, yet their eradication offers opportunities for great evolutionary leaps. One has only to think of social sins—such as racism, prejudice, poverty, disease, exploitation of the poor, gender inequality, abuse of the planet's resources, greed-driven capitalism, nuclear threats, and many other divisive social structures—to realize how much we take them for granted, even as we recognize their powerful hindrances to renewing the face of Earth with love.[84]

There are still people who would lie and cheat and defraud others of their money and possessions. There are still people who believe that violence and war is the only way to peace and harmony. There are still people who are committed to seeking revenge and meting out unjust punishment. There are still people who are determined to disrupt human progress and development. There are still people who refuse to make their contribution to God's project. There are still people who are content to remain critics, complainers, bystanders, loafers, spongers, and so on. While there are people that continue to act in these ways, the completion of God's project is further delayed.

In many ways, people in all these examples, though they may have brilliant minds, are essentially ethically immature persons. They are still stuck in a self-focused mentality. They have never experienced a moral mindset shift.

The most insidious harm is done to our human community by what are called *social sins*.[85] Each of us, to some degree, participates in, supports, condones, or at least tolerates these social sins by our action and inaction. None of us is exempt. Mostly, we do it unconsciously and by inaction.

Social Sin: An Infestation

While personal sins of omission, one might argue, leave empty or unfinished spaces in the necessary evolutionary work of building a loving mansion for God on Earth, social sins act more like an infestation of termites in God's building. Termites usually infiltrate an entire building, quietly eating away at it. Their destructive activity usually remains unnoticed until the devastation becomes painfully evident.

Social sins are those quiet and mostly unnoticed destructive behaviors common to the community that diminish all-embracing love among groups of people and continually break apart society's unity and organization. Although some of these socially corrosive practices are sometimes reflected in local, state, and federal laws, most often they are more like insidious unspoken agreements among groups of people to dislike or reject certain other groups of people.

Two obvious subtle unspoken agreements still operating in the United States are what might be called "white privilege" and "male privilege." For many years, well into the twentieth century, home realtors quietly agreed—or were required—to do racial profiling, to keep black people from buying homes in predominantly white middle-class neighborhoods. The whites' excuse for this unfair practice of racial segregation was to "maintain the value of our homes."

"Male privilege" may be expressed, for example, by offering preferential treatment to men over women in hiring practices, job promotion, and higher wages. White male privilege is a combination of both.

Charles Curran, one of the most outstanding moral theologians of our time, recently wrote an essay about his only lately becoming aware of his own unconscious racism and white privilege. He wrote,

> I have to face the reality that I barely recognized the problem of racism in my own somewhat extensive writings and was blithely unaware of my own white privilege….White privilege functions invisibly and systematically to confer power and privilege. Only very recently have I been educated to realize the extent and power of white privilege and my participation in it.[86]

If a prominent moral theologian remained essentially unaware of his own biases, how much more unaware must the rest of us be?

Many common social sins contribute to a contagious viral infection of a society trying to remain healthy while growing in peace and love. Among these societal infections are racial profiling, sexual discrimination, human slavery, unjust treatment of immigrants and refugees, ethnic cleansing, unbridled capitalism, the exaltation of wealth, religious bias, unfair employment practices, glorified militarism, financial manipulation of poorer nations, acceptance of graft in governmental organizations, acceptance of gratuitous violence and sexuality in the media, inequity in education and health care, unbridled nepotism, unjust wages, exploitation of child labor, drug abuse, consciously creating poverty among the poor, white supremacy, paternalism, patriarchy, misuse of nature's bounty, pollution of lakes and rivers, and environmental pollution.

Most of these social sins are perpetuated by powerful people, organizations, and governments to maintain their dominance and control of others. It is difficult to love your brothers and sisters if you really want to control and dominate them — or pity them. Pity, too, can be a cruel emotion — at any level of society — when it causes "helpers" to feel superior or better than those they help.

Spiritual Exercise: Confronting Social Sin

Have you ever tried, even in a small way, to confront a social sin embedded in your workplace, your neighborhood, or your church? What was the response you received? Have you ever been in a situation where you saw how you could confront a social sin, but refrained from acting?

Built-In Social Sin

Social sin describes the immoral habits of the society into which a person is born. Social sin is "systemic," which means it is a built-in structure of our society that doesn't promote the kingdom of God. No matter how loving and holy our parents might have been, we were born immersed in the larger society's collective unjust values and immoral actions. This powerful immersion happened so thoroughly and so early in life that we were often unaware of it, for example, the acceptance of white privilege in America and male privilege throughout the world.

Social sin is quietly but effectively structured into our social behavior. Social sin is the cumulative result of thousands or even millions of different preferential choices made consistently over time by many different individuals. When such collective destructive practices become customary and acceptable, and their harmful effects are spread over the larger community or society in general, it is called "social sin."

Slavery and racial discrimination are good examples of social sins. Early in the history of the United States, a small group of landowners decided to buy slaves to run their farms. At first, other landowners were upset by this practice and felt it was immoral. But, eventually when they saw their slave-owning neighbor producing more crops, they began to rationalize the practice and decided to buy some slaves themselves. Perhaps, they said to themselves, "As long as we treat our slaves well, slavery isn't really bad. After all, there have been slaves in the world as long as people can remember." Soon, many in the American South—and some in the North—were practicing slavery and pleased with the abundance of their production. Slavery soon became an essential structure in the nation's economy. Thus, the personal and collective demeaning of the liberties of an entire racial group, socially and financially, became acceptable.

The social sin of racism and slavery even reached into religious institutions. For example, in 1789, before the Emancipation Proclamation, Jesuit superiors at Georgetown University brought to the school almost three hundred African American slaves from Jesuit plantations in Maryland to help with the construction of university buildings in the nation's capital. In 1838, other Jesuit superiors at the university sold 272 of their slaves for profit to keep the university financially afloat.[87]

In 2016, nearly two centuries later, Georgetown University's president acknowledged that the university had embarked on a series of steps to atone for its past sins. Among the self-assigned penances, the university would begin offering preferential status in the admission process to descendants of the enslaved, create an institute for the study of slavery, and erect a public memorial on campus to honor the slaves whose labor benefited the institution.

More than a dozen other universities, including Brown, Harvard, and the University of Virginia, have publicly recognized their ties to slavery and the slave trade.[88]

Social sin, once it becomes habitual in a community, endures and grows. What may have seemed unethical a generation ago now seems socially acceptable and financially necessary. The devaluing of blacks was subtly enshrined in our Constitution, where each black male was to be counted as three-fifths of a white male. In elections, each of those three-fifths persons counted as three-fifths of a vote, and their "votes" were cast by the one white male who owned them.

Here's another example of social sin. In Hollywood of the 1950s, nudity or unnecessary depiction of sexual activity was unacceptable in the film industry. In early movies, even married couples wore modest pajamas and slept in separate twin beds. Vile language was also unacceptable. No cursing, swearing, or using God's name as an expletive. But the industry realized that people would be more inclined to go to movies that displayed some gratuitous sexual activity on the screen. The same went for the unnecessary depiction of violence, the gorier the better. The same went for vulgar language, the cruder the better. Gradually, the social barriers dropped further, so that movie audiences today are almost inured to viewing graphic violence, crude language, and explicit sexuality. Today, such imagery is taken for granted as the social norm. Many Hollywood and television producers continue to find more ways to exploit sexuality, violence, and foul language. They justify their behavior by saying, "That's what people want."

Self-centeredness and personal entitlement are two other social sins that have become acceptable. We can walk by poor or homeless people on the street without any feeling of compassion. So-called upright citizens may even demand that laws be made to keep such people off the streets, so that they do not have to be seen. Better to arrest them than have them visible. "Don't give them welfare money, for they will only use it to by alcohol, cigarettes, or drugs. Why should I lift a hand to help them? I need my customized latte each morning, and I'm tired of my old mattress, so I'll buy the newest expensive model. And I certainly need the latest smartphone."

Each time we vote for candidates who consistently cut social programs to the poor, and each time we purchase products from corporations who pay substandard wages, we contribute to the social sin of poverty and self-centeredness.

Someone had the powerful insight that social sin often results from selfish *omissions* rather than selfish acts. Rather than confront social sin, we say or do nothing.

It is easy to see why mainstream Christianity focuses on individual sin rather than on social sin. Sin that is structured into the social system is more difficult to understand and identify. It is more difficult to remove since it has become common and, for some, acceptable behavior. In many cases, social sin has been institutionalized in various laws, customs, and practices, making it more difficult to eradicate. Besides, who wants to fight society?

Our contribution to social sin is no less sinful than our individual misdeeds. Some may claim that sinful social structures enjoy a life completely divorced from individuals' decisions or intentions, thereby blaming institutions or systems, not individuals, for social evils. This is *not* a true understanding of social sin. Indeed, social sin—as the sum of countless selfish actions and omissions[89]—is, in the long run, *more* destructive and damaging to God's project than individual sin. It pollutes the atmosphere where love is trying to grow.

So where do we go from here? How do we undo social sin and go forward with God's project? Most people seem to understand how individual sin can be addressed, namely, by repentance, contrition, confession, and so on. But, how does a community repent and change its ways regarding social sin? Unfortunately, Teilhard doesn't give us a specific program to follow. Perhaps Georgetown University's public atonement regarding slavery offers a small example of accepting responsibility.

In general, the first step in eradicating social sin is to realize and acknowledge how our individual decisions contribute to it, and to do our part incrementally to change it. As Mahatma Gandhi said, "Be the change you want to see in the world." Obviously, we can choose to consume less and give more to charity, vote for those who support social programs for the poor, take a job that effects social change, volunteer. No one can disagree with those steps.

But is there anything more profound and permanent we can help to accomplish? Perhaps to support and join a prophetic, grassroots movement that calls us to a better way?

Spiritual Exercise: Difficult to Eradicate

Which of the following social sins have been the most difficult for you to become conscious of your participation in?

- *racial prejudice* (e.g., toward blacks)
- *religious or ethnic prejudice* (e.g., toward Jews or Muslims)
- *gender prejudice* (e.g., toward lesbians, gays, transgender persons)
- *military warfare* (e.g., as a solution of terrorism)
- *gratuitous violence* (e.g., in film and television)
- *gratuitous sexuality* (e.g., in film and television)
- *abusive behavior toward children and women* (especially in the home)
- *special preference for the wealthy* (e.g., showing them more respect than the poor)
- *male privilege* (e.g., male entitlement in the home, church, workplace, and society)
- *reverence of money* (e.g., willingness to deceive, lie, or cheat in money matters)

ETHICAL PRINCIPLE 10:
Spiritual Maturity and Consciousness

People operate morally at many different levels of spiritual maturity and consciousness. *(Derived from Basic Principles 1, 2, 5, 6, 7, 8)*

It is important to remember that a person's ethical decisions are often made from within a certain level of conscious development. In any family or professional group, its members may be operating at various stages of spiritual maturity or levels of consciousness. As a result, each person may be making choices based on different perceptions of ethical rules or beliefs.

As Teilhard discovered, even people within the same organization may not be operating at the same degree of moral maturity. He discovered that fact very strikingly in his dealings with church authorities in Rome.[90]

Developmental Levels

Psychologists have identified several major moral and emotional developmental levels through which people normally grow. They have also identified certain ages at which people typically graduate from one level to the next. Some people, naturally and according to schedule, move through two or three levels in their own personal evolutionary process toward emotional and ethical maturity. Others seem to get stuck at one or other moral level of development and continue through life operating from within the values or moral criteria at that level.

There seems to be little correlation between intellectual development and emotional and moral maturity. One may be highly developed intellectually yet operate morally like a two-year-old child or a middle-school student, whose desires and wishes are mostly self-focused. Here is a quick sketch of some major stages or levels of moral development.

Level One. The earliest moral level might be called the *reward or punishment stage.* This is typically observed in young children, who quickly learn that they are rewarded for good behavior. The reward may be a smile of approval, a hug, or a kiss — or possibly a piece of candy or another treat. Likewise, they learn very quickly which behaviors earn parental disapproval or punishment. Level One is a very self-focused stage. Although we all go through life enjoying approval and trying to avoid disapproval, most mature adults do not make moral choices depending on whether they'll be rewarded or punished for them. Usually, grownups have developed higher motives for their choices and actions.

However, there are certain adults whose moral consciences still operate primarily according to the expectation of *reward or punishment.* Morally and ethically, they are still self-focused at Level One. They will behave in socially appropriate ways only when it is in their self-interest. That is, reward and punishment remain the major factors that motivate such people to act morally and ethically. They will lie, cheat, avoid responsibility, take advantage of the weak and vulnerable, provided they don't get caught. In Florida, there are several thieves who regularly steal another person's identity, file an income tax return in that person's name, and have the overpayment check sent to the thief's address. Other self-centered people might say, "It's okay for me to do this, as long as I can get away with it." They are operating at Level One.

Level Two. Typically, when children reach middle-school age, they develop a second moral level called the *obedience or duty* stage. They discover there are social rules of behavior expected of everyone. They learn to cooperate with these rules because they realize it is the best way for them to get along peacefully with others. They are no longer driven primarily by reward or punishment. Rather, they wish to obey social rules because it is their *duty* to do so. They discover there are rules for good health, such as not smoking. At this age, they may encourage a relative who doesn't vote to do their civic duty. They discover there are rules for safety, and so will encourage adult drivers to put on their seat belts. They discover there are rules for using proper grammar, doing mathematics, playing computer games, participating in sports, giving gifts, making and keeping friends, and so on. There are rules that govern almost every activity, not only in childhood but also throughout life. Living by social and religious rules is most characteristic of Level Two.

Even though there are higher levels of moral consciousness, there are still many adults who stop moral development at Level Two. Morally, they continue to operate primarily out of a *sense of duty.* For them, one of the highest moral values is to be obedient to authority. "If the church tells me to do this or that, I will obey. If my employer or my government tells me to do this or that, I obey. If my political party tells me how to vote, that is what I will do." There is nothing wrong with fulfilling one's religious, legal, and public obligations. But it is basically a relatively immature moral position simply to manage your life based on the rules or regulations of an organization. Adults who remain stuck at the "duty" stage are still not in charge of their personal choices and behavior because this ethical position does not require a person to develop a personal moral conscience. Authorities and their assigned duties make moral decisions for them.

Level Three. Somewhere around high-school age, many young people move into a third moral stage based on *logic or reason.* They begin to question certain social customs or behaviors of the adults around them and ask, *Why?* "What is the reason behind this rule, custom, or law?" This is an age at which young adults begin to recognize the prejudices or biases of the grownups around them and may choose to behave differently. They decide to do something because they personally have thought about it, and to them it seems right. Likewise, they will choose not to do something because they have concluded that it is wrong. While the middle-school student might hesitate to question any authority or custom, the high-school student at this third level of moral development finds it natural to question imposed behavior and even to challenge it. If they are expected to obey a social or religious rule, they want to know why they should comply. They insist on a reasonable explanation. To a young person at Level Three, it is no longer sufficient for a parent to say, "You'll do it because I say so."

Many adults operate primarily at this third developmental level. They make choices out of *logic or reason.* People at this level will normally comply with an ethical rule that seems reasonable but may question anything that seems unreasonable or unprovable. They will believe something if it makes sense to them. Religiously, these are the people who may listen to a Sunday sermon, but disagree with what was said because it seemed to them not to make good sense. They might say to their spouse, "The pastor doesn't have his facts straight on that issue."

It is interesting to note that someone fixated in Level Two often cannot understand how someone at Level Three could challenge the rationality of a religious or civil law. A pastor (operating at Level Two) may be convinced that he (or she) is right because the Bible—or the bishop or the pope—says something is true and cannot imagine anyone disagreeing with religious authority. Similarly, people entering Level Three often cannot understand how anyone could remain at Level Two, without questioning the reasonableness of the pastor's words, when the pastor is acting solely in obedience to an outside authority.

Level Four. There is still a higher level of moral development that the psychologists talk about. We might call it a *personal moral conscience* stage. There are people who have, over the years, developed a personal moral conscience that guides them in deciding what they should or should not do in any given situation. This level goes beyond the concern for reason, rationality, and accuracy of facts that characterize Stage Three. Those at Level Four have developed *their own set of moral and ethical principles.* Some of these principles may correspond with social customs, religious doctrines, and various authorities, but others may be principles they have come to believe and live by that don't agree with the way others think. Many of these principles are altruistic, that is, such people accept responsibility for the welfare of others, not merely for themselves and their loved ones. People who have reached this fourth stage of moral development have accepted responsibility for developing the moral principles that guide their lives.

One identifying mark for those at Level Four is their willingness to accept the consequences of their own decisions. During the Vietnam War, there were conscientious objectors to military service who believed the United States was engaged in an unjust war and refused to participate in it, even if they were drafted. They were willing to accept the legal and social consequences of their decision.

Teilhard himself offers another good example of this *personal moral conscience* stage.[91] He wrote about how he had developed his own personal moral conscience integrating science and evolution with Christian theology and recognizing some of its moral implications. But he was forbidden by his church to publish or teach his ideas. Although he tried to explain their validity and value to Vatican officials, they refused to listen.[92] At the time, the institutional church took a very defensive position regarding modern science and evolution.[93] As a faithful son of the church and his religious order, he abided by their restrictions not to publish. He accepted the consequences, yet he continued until his death to write essays integrating theology and evolution with Christian doctrine. While some of these writings were copied and shared among friends, many remained unpublished until after his death.

Our daily newspaper includes two advice columns, written by women who are clearly operating at Level Four. One of the hallmarks of people at this level is that they recognize and understand those who are operating at lower levels and know how to approach them. Level Four people can empathize with people transitioning to the next level while struggling with those they love who are at a lower level. In a recent advice column in "Dear Abby," a teenage girl growing into Level Three fears that she will upset her "religious" mother (operating at Level Two) if she says what she thinks.

The young woman disagrees with some things her parents think are sinful. She writes, "I want to support gay rights and animal rights. My mother, in particular, takes the Bible literally, while I am more open. I want to support these causes, but I'm afraid she will be angry. Please help me."

Abby's response is very wise. "Be patient. There is no way to change the thinking of someone who takes the Bible—or any holy book, for that matter—literally. Do what you can now, but you may have to wait until you are older and on your own to become fully active in these causes."[94]

Essentially, the columnist is saying that if someone is committed to living their lives at Level Two, there is not much anyone can do about it, except to be patient and understanding. Such people may even believe that at Level Two they are operating at the highest moral level, and anyone who thinks differently is wrong and, for that matter, immoral.

Imagine the difficulty of a workplace supervisor who, on his intellectually bright team, has members who are each operating at various levels of moral development. To team members at Level One, the supervisor must offer frequent praise (reward) for any work done well and propose threats (punishment) for any work done poorly or submitted late. To members at Level Two, the supervisor must make clear all the rules and regulations that are to be followed in the task. To members at Level Three, the supervisor will get best support if he or she explains the logic and reasoning behind any assignments given. The supervisor can usually count on any team members at Level Four to recognize the levels at which others are operating and support the supervisor appropriately and quietly.

Spiritual Exercise: Mixing Levels of Consciousness

In the example above, it is assumed that the supervisor is operating at Level Four. Can you suggest the responses of team members from each level, if the supervisor is operating only at Level Two?

Higher Levels of Consciousness

In our age of individualism, this fourth stage of *personal moral conscience* defined by the psychologists seems to be the highest, generally recognized level of moral maturity for a human person.

Teilhard suggests there are even higher stages of moral development that psychologists have not mentioned, such as developing a planetary conscience or even a cosmic conscience.

Level Five. One higher level, *planetary consciousness*, is a stage of moral development where one accepts responsibility to do all one can for the survival, health, and development of Earth itself.[95] Teilhard was already operating at this stage in 1920, though few others at the time seemed to recognize planetary consciousness as a higher ethical stage of moral development. Teilhard says this level is, at present, "the most complex and the most unified state human consciousness has yet attained."[96]

Eckhart Tolle, a contemporary spiritual teacher, captured a sense of this fifth stage beginning to happen:

> In many parts of the world, there is an emerging sense of social justice that our ancestors couldn't even have dreamed of. The subjugation of one race by another, the domination of women throughout thousands of years of patriarchy, and the devaluing of people based on social class are for growing numbers of us nightmares of the past. People of different gender orientations find themselves increasingly accepted simply as people. The races marry and intermingle with less and less judgment. There is a growing awareness of the intrinsic oneness of everything that exists, so that more and more we are seeing an awareness of and deep concern for our fellow humans, the countless animals that are our traveling companions, and the planet itself. Such awareness implies that there is indeed a lessening of the ego in a growing number of people, and in some parts of the planet more than in others. This diminishment of the ego gives rise to empathy and compassion beyond tribal, racial, national, or religious affiliations. It is those qualities that make us truly human.[97]

In planetary consciousness, people see themselves as morally responsible, not merely for themselves, but for the entire planet, including everyone and everything on it. Such people are not ego-centered, and not merely other-centered, but are geo-centered.

For Teilhard, the main evolutionary concern for God's project in our time is getting people to reach Level Five. He saw this step as crucial for the evolutionary process to continue developing. It includes doing whatever one could, alone and in teams, to forward the evolutionary movement toward God.

This geo-centered spirituality and morality is clearly described in Teilhard's memoir that he called "Mass on the World." When Teilhard lifted up the bread offering at Mass, he saw in the consecrated host not merely Jesus Christ, but all human beings whose activity and struggles this day were being spent to renew the face of Earth. And when he lifted up the blessed chalice, he saw not merely the blood of Jesus Christ but the sufferings and diminishments of all the people and creatures on Earth that would happen on this day.[98] Already in 1920, Teilhard was celebrating Mass with planetary consciousness.

A century later, in 2015, Pope Francis in his encyclical *Laudato Si': On Care for Our Common Home*) for the first time outlined this new level of planetary moral conscience. In his encyclical, he sketches some of the scope of this new moral stage:

> The urgent challenge to protect our common home includes a concern to bring the whole human family together to seek a sustainable and integral development, for we know that things can change. The Creator does not abandon us; he never forsakes his loving plan or repents of having created us. Humanity still has the ability to work together in building our common home. Here I want to recognize, encourage and thank all those striving in countless ways to guarantee the protection of the home that we share. Particular appreciation is owed to those who tirelessly seek to resolve the tragic effects of environmental degradation on the lives of the world's poorest. Young people demand change. They wonder how anyone can claim to be building a better future without thinking of the environmental crisis and the sufferings of the excluded. (no. 13)

Level Six. Teilhard had also reached—and taught—an even higher, _cosmic level of moral development_ in his recognition of God's project and Christogenesis. For Teilhard, Christogenesis revealed a bigger picture, what we might call the conscience or consciousness of Christ the Lord of the cosmos.[99] The Cosmic Christ is concerned, not merely about planet Earth, but also about the more than 100 billion galaxies swirling in our grand universe. Not just planet Earth, but also the entire universe lives in the "divine milieu." The entire universe is alive in Christ. For Teilhard, the grand evolutionary vision of the Creator is to bring the entire universe together in love.[100] He writes, "To cooperate in total cosmic evolution is the only deliberate act that can adequately express our devotion to an evolutive and universal Christ."[101]

We humans have our moral developmental work cut out for us on Earth. We each must do our own part to promote Christogenesis on Earth during our lifetime. But Christ's visionary task is far greater. It involves the entire universe. The universe provides a much larger sense of "home" than our planet Earth. Since we are parts of Christ's evolving body (Christogenesis includes the entire cosmos). Wherever Christ is, that is our home. For example, within our grandchildren's lifetime, the planet Mars will likely become "home" for some space voyagers.

Teilhard recognized the potential for developing this cosmic conscience in his book _The Divine Milieu_.[102]

It is very difficult for most of us living at one of the four lower levels of moral development to even envision developing a "planetary conscience," let alone a "cosmic conscience." Yet, there are some today who are calling for humanity to develop a sense of union with the whole cosmos, to see the "big picture" and recognize the universe as our "common home."

In a recent talk, Teilhardian scholar Ilia Delio quoted two such authors who were calling for a cosmic conscience. They wrote, "There is a gaping hole in modern thinking: we have no meaningful sense of how we and our fellow humans fit into the big picture….Without a big picture we are very small people."[103]

Teilhard would say that, for us contemporary humans, the first challenge is probably to strive to develop a planetary moral conscience. We need such an expanded conscience to be aware enough and committed enough to deal with the global crises we face today, religiously, militarily, financially, and ecologically.[104]

In a Teilhardian system, each person is morally responsible according to his or her level of moral development. And each is expected to mature in moral responsibility.

People operate at various levels of spiritual maturity and consciousness. We need to learn to recognize people operating at each of the first four levels of consciousness and respond to them at that level, while encouraging them to evolve into a next level, just as we try to evolve to a higher level.

Spiritual Exercise: Levels of Consciousness

It is consoling to know that no matter at what level of consciousness we may happen to be, we are able to grow and develop beyond it, and furthermore, to know that God loves us unconditionally at whatever moral level we are operating presently. Can you name some people or organizations where the members share a "planetary consciousness"?

ETHICAL PRINCIPLE 11:
A Major Purpose for Acts of Healing, Forgiveness, and Mercy

A major purpose for acts of healing, forgiveness, mercy—toward the sick, grieving, rejected, orphans, widows, the unemployed, and so on—is to enable recipients of our care to rejoin the community so that they may make their unique loving contribution to God's project. (*Derived from Basic Principles 3, 4, 5, 6, 7, 8*)

Consider the varieties of pain and fever that, for millennia, have kept people at home, in bed or unable to function effectively, unable to make their unique loving contribution to God's project.

Then think of the most universal and readily available over-the-counter pain-relieving, fever-lowering, and anti-inflammatory medication that has been used, in one form or another, by tens of millions of people worldwide every day for over a hundred years, so that they could make their unique loving contribution to God's project. I am referring to *aspirin*.

The aspirin tablet was first patented in the United States in 1900 by Bayer Pharmaceuticals. Its inventor, a German chemist named

Felix Hoffman, is said to have synthesized it to help his father, who found the medicine prescribed for his rheumatism too acidic. The Bayer Company, for whom Hoffman worked, realized the almost limitless potential for healing offered by this medicine. Aspirin was perhaps the first medication in history to be manufactured and sold in this now-universally familiar, water-soluble tablet form.

When we look at the many healings Jesus did during his public life, it seems clear that he was not doing them primarily to make an impression on the crowds or to prove that he was divine. He was healing people of their pain and afflictions so that, no longer blind, deaf, or crippled, they could return to their communities and be better able to make their contribution to family and social life. He was making them "whole" again, giving them a fuller life.

That God wanted us to have the fullness of life was the gospel message, the good news. The kingdom of God was present, and it was an unconditional loving and healing presence. Even though only one of ten healed lepers came back to thank Jesus, all of them were healed and remained healed. God's love was and remains unconditional (see Luke 17:11–19).

We are called to see "sinners," not as "bad" but rather as personally weak, emotionally immature, or morally underdeveloped (unripe). To help such people gain personal self-control, develop emotionally, and grow in moral consciousness remains a continually important human work for God's project. The hope is that, as people mature emotionally and morally, they may better contribute to the growth of the world in love.

If you helped anyone in their physical, psychological, or spiritual growth, you were living out this eleventh principle. For example, perhaps you

- contributed to a scholarship fund for students from poor families
- tutored children struggling with a school subject
- served on a research team finding a new life-giving drug
- drove someone every morning to the cancer center for radiation treatments
- as a pharmacist, gave flu shots to keep people healthy during flu season

- as a law enforcement officer, prevented a murder
- as a firefighter, saved an elderly person from a burning building
- volunteered in Habitat for Humanity to help build a home for a poor family
- planted a garden in your backyard and shared your produce with your neighbors
- lobbied your state legislature to raise the minimum wage
- gave money to a foster mother of three handicapped children, so she could get the special eyeglasses she needed for driving at night
- counseled people with mental or emotional problems
- as a school nurse, consoled children who had fallen and bruised themselves on the playground
- as a professor, wrote letters of recommendation for students seeking admission to graduate school

There are thousands of ways that people in their everyday activities can help others to enjoy "more life" and make their contributions to the community.

Spiritual Exercise: Giving Back to the Community

Can you think of times when you helped someone have a fuller life by an act of kindness, healing, forgiveness, or mercy?

Conclusion

When presented with the option to evolve morally, most people may not want to change in Teilhard's way. They may not even want to try. It may seem to them to be too great a challenge to make the radical shift from seeing themselves as ordinary human beings to seeing themselves as members of a planetary team engaged in working on God's project. They may hesitate to accept and develop their potential capacities to cooperate consciously in this great undertaking. Perhaps they see it as an impossible challenge to change their self-perception, metaphorically, from being a caterpillar to becoming a butterfly. Learning to fly is scary.

Some have suggested that many don't want to evolve morally because they feel they would fail — or not be good enough. They have already failed at many things: some couldn't lose weight; some couldn't stop smoking; some couldn't change annoying habits; some couldn't develop deep, lasting relationships; some couldn't conquer self-doubt; some couldn't develop self-confidence. They are now afraid that, even if they try to evolve morally, they will not be able to fly like a butterfly.

Recognizing the inherent weaknesses in people, traditional morality built itself around sin and forgiveness and encouraged people to invest their efforts in achieving their salvation (fullness of life) only after death. They would reach this goal by doing the good works expected of them, seeking forgiveness of their sins, and placing their hope in God's mercy at the time of death.

Death is a natural ending we all must face. Unlike animals, human beings can think about death, especially their own death. Human awareness of death is meant to be an awakening. The conscious thought of death is meant to wake us up, capture our attention, and force us to reflect upon how we are living and how we want to live. Death demands that we take our life seriously. Being alive is a profound mystery and a precious gift.

In traditional morality, your life's purpose is to save your individual soul. In contrast, in an evolutionary morality, your life's purpose is to use your abilities, talents, and resources, while you are on Earth, to work courageously to transform our earthly home and the people on it. Your life purpose is to work to help further God's project, to move creation forward.

In Teilhard's approach, mortality becomes an evolutionary challenge "to live with more intensity, intimacy, immensity and intentionality."[105] It is to live less like a caterpillar, who can see only a few feet of the ground around him, and more like a butterfly, who can see a vast and beautiful world.

Using this metaphor, Teilhard would say that it is our nature and destiny to fly. And we can learn how to do it. We have not been given life to remain living as lowly creatures unable to focus on little more than ourselves and our own weakness, vulnerability, and helplessness. Rather, Teilhard tells us that we are each called to live with one another sharing a higher perspective. We are the ones on Earth that can imagine the potential grandeur waiting to be gradually realized in all of creation. We are called to live, here and now, with a passionate love for creation and an intense desire to work together in helping God accomplish the grand project that God has started on Earth.

Appendix

Teilhard on Original Sin and Baptism

THE ROMAN CATHOLIC Church silenced Teilhard de Chardin primarily because of his position on original sin and his outspoken promotion of the theory of evolution as it affected original sin. Because of Teilhard's nontraditional explanation of sin, its origins and its effects, he was forbidden to publish his theological and philosophical books and papers. He was also ordered not to lecture or teach his theological ideas in public.

For almost two thousand years, the church accepted the first chapters of the Book of Genesis as a definitive foundation of the Christian doctrines regarding the origins of human life, sin, suffering, and death in the world.[1] Forgiveness of that "original sin" plus all the other sins that humans have committed since then was seen by most theologians as a primary reason for Jesus's redemptive suffering and death on the cross. In church teaching, Adam's sin and Jesus's death were intimately linked. To challenge the centrality of Adam's sin, as Teilhard was doing, would be to the challenge the significance of our redemption in Jesus Christ, according to the church.

In Teilhard's day, geologists and anthropologists were making startling discoveries regarding the evolution of various life forms on Earth including humans. The church, however, preferred to avoid dealing with any evidence that might challenge the Genesis story. It especially maintained Adam's transgression as the source of all sin, suffering, evil, and death. At the time, there was such fear among the church hierarchy from the many new revelations of science, that the pope felt it important to maintain the literal interpretation of the Genesis Creation stories, especially that of Adam and Eve and the perfect Garden of

151

Eden that God had prepared for them. As a result, the church rejected many findings of contemporary science that had to do with evolution, especially any interpretation of those findings that challenged the biblical account of our first parents.[2] Such scientific findings were lumped together and labeled as a heretical teaching called "modernism." It was defined and condemned by Pope Pius X in 1907.[3] Beginning in 1910 and for the next fifty years, every Catholic priest and seminarian was required to swear an oath against modernism.[4]

Original Sin and the Catechism

The *Catechism of the Catholic Church* clearly states that, although we are all burdened by the effects of original sin, *original sin is not a personal sin*. It's not a sin that you and I commit—or ever committed. A personal sin is an act that a person knows is morally forbidden yet consciously chooses to do it. Thus, an infant cannot commit a sin. That is why the *Catechism* carefully says of original sin, "It is a sin 'contracted' and not 'committed'—a state and not an act" (CCC 404).

According to church teachings, original sin is a "state" into which every person is born. This "state" is described as an inherited weakened condition of our natural powers. From its beginnings, according to the doctrine, this weakened condition and tendency to sin has been continuously passed on from parent to child through all the ages of humanity.

Theologically, original sin is described as a condition of "human nature deprived of original holiness and justice" (CCC 404). In traditional theology, the assumption is that the very first humans, Adam and Eve, were created *without original sin*. They were created without this weakness and tendency to sin because it is also assumed in traditional theology that God cannot create anything that is imperfect.

Before the discovery of evolution, no theologian even considered that God could use a third option and create humans as "beings in process," which is a much more accurate description of humanity, individually and collectively. Each of us individually is a person in process. The human species is also going through a collective developmental process. As Teilhard points out, even the Body of Christ is in process

(Christogenesis). For Teilhard, though we are all "imperfect," we are also all "in process" toward a higher state.

According to church tradition, following the text of the first chapters of Genesis, the first humans were created as fully mature adults with a nature that was pure and holy. Adam and Eve were presumed to have all powers that were appropriate to God's image of civilized human beings. That tradition says that it was the personal sin of our first parents that permanently marred and weakened our originally "perfect" human nature.

Despite the enduring effects of that first personal sin, the *Catechism* teaches, our human nature is not "totally corrupted," but is merely "wounded." Because of this wound deep in our nature, every human person's natural powers are "subject to ignorance, suffering and the dominion of death, and inclined to sin—an inclination to evil that is called concupiscence" (no. 405).[5]

In the end, the *Catechism* acknowledges, "The transmission of original sin is a mystery that we cannot fully understand" (no. 404).

The Adam and Eve Story

Teilhard had difficulty with the story of Adam and Eve, especially with its implications regarding sin. He had two crucial issues with it.

The first issue was with the biblical explanation as to *how so much pain and suffering entered the world after one human action.*

According to the Book of Genesis, two perfect, sinless, yet naive human beings, Adam and Eve, were put to the test. They were told not to eat of the fruit of a certain tree. They were tempted to disobey God's command and, unfortunately, they acted on that temptation. The cumulative negative effects of this single act of disobedience on all future human beings became immense. Those effects were passed on to all of us—and to all creation—in a never-ending succession of generations.[6]

The evil effects[7] of that one sin include pain, suffering, sickness, disease, abnormality, accidents, mistakes, confusion, conflicts, isolation, rejection, loss, disorder, decay, corruption, exposure, death, failures, dangers, loss from harmful weather events such as tornados, floods, droughts, freezes, and eruptions.

Like us, Teilhard was aware of the prevalence of these evils among us then and today. His problem was that Scripture had them originating *only after Adam and Eve's first sin* (about six thousand years ago according to the Bible). Dinosaurs elimination

Based on scientific evidence, Teilhard asserted these unwelcome effects had been present in the universe from its origins over thirteen billion years ago and on Earth from its origins over four billion years ago. The list of evil effects described above may be considered merely human evils from our perspective, but they are all part and parcel of an evolving universe. Suffering, confusion, conflict, and even death are unavoidable and inescapable in an evolutionary process that is only gradually finding its way forward in growing complexity and consciousness.[8]

Teilhard's second issue with the Adam and Eve sin was that it was *too narrow, too local.*[9] According to Catholic theology, this sin and its effects involved only humanity. But as we know, creation—the universe—is far larger in scope than humanity and planet Earth. Even on Earth, the evolutionary process had been struggling forward— and suffering—for hundreds of millions of years before the advent of humans. Everything has always been groaning with the pain of growth and development.

As St. Paul recognized, we humans are not the only ones who live and move and have our being in Christ. Nothing that exists—or ever existed—can exist outside of the universal or Cosmic Christ, the Lord of the Universe. In him all things come together (see Col 1:17). So, for Teilhard, to limit the effects of original sin to the human family conflicts with the cosmos-sized reality of the universal Christ that we encounter in our theological tradition. Teilhard wrote, "If, therefore, we are to have an atmosphere in which we can breathe, we must make a fresh approach to the problem of evil in its relationship to Christ, and rethink it in terms that fit in with our new cosmic views."[10]

What Teilhard Faced

The above medieval approach to original sin was what Teilhard was taught as a child in his catechism classes as well as in his Jesuit theological studies. He encountered difficulties with this approach when he began reflecting on the origins of original sin in terms of geological discoveries. A problem he faced was the growing evidence ____ concerning the evolutionary origins of *Homo sapiens*. There was no clear-cut evidence about how early it was in the evolution of *Homo* that self-reflective beings emerged who could consciously commit sin. Certainly, the now-extinct Neanderthals had been a self-reflective people. Our species and the Neanderthals shared planet Earth for many thousands of years. Did the Neanderthals possess a consciousness capable of committing sin and a conscience to recognize it for what it was?

Moreover, Teilhard knew that, eons before the first humans took____ their first breath, those unwelcome "effects of original sin," such as suffering and death, were already a very common experience in plants, animals, and pre-human hominins. Teilhard was forced to look for the "origins" of original sin far deeper in time than when Adam and Eve were said to be walking in their lovely garden.

It is important to note that, for Teilhard, Christogenesis (the Cosmic Body of Christ still in its painful developmental process) was always the principal factor in his considerations, both theological and moral. Moreover, his theological approach to Christ always had a forward, developmental thrust. Like St. Paul, Teilhard was more concerned about the healthy future of the Body of Christ, the Cosmic and universal Christ, than he was about the Jesus who walked the dusty roads of Galilee.[11] Teilhard was always looking to what the Body of Christ was becoming and could yet become. The Body of Christ was __ still developing, still gestating. For Teilhard, we are living in a period of process that is Christogenesis. His focus was always on Christogenesis. It was central in his re-envisioning of original sin.

Re-envisioning Original Sin

Even though original sin is an important dogma of the church, Teilhard recognized that it is not the central dogma. The church's central and primary dogma is and has always been the mystery of Christ. Therefore, Teilhard needed to find a way of re-envisioning original sin ____ that was integrated more fully with the more important church doctrines about Christ—creation, incarnation, redemption, and the fulfillment of Christ at the end of time. He wrote several essays in which he explained this integrative approach to original sin.[12]

Teilhard has been accused of denying original sin. He never denied it. He found the traditional medieval interpretation of original sin—a sin of Adam and Eve that affected only humanity—very limiting. It was limiting because *all creation,* as St. Paul recognized, is burdened by the effects of original sin in much the same way as humans are (see Rom 8:19–23). What Teilhard did was *to enlarge the scope of original sin,* because its wider scope is central to an understanding of church doctrines about Christ in light of an evolving creation.

In his explorations of original sin from an evolutionary perspective, *Teilhard's primary purpose was to integrate the doctrine of original sin into an overall Christian vision of reality as the universe is understood today by science.*

He wanted to create a vision that (1) would recognize the importance of development of the entire created world in the fulfillment of Christ (Christogenesis or God's project); and (2) would show the responsibility humans, especially Christians, have in helping Christ achieve that fulfillment (Christogenesis).

Both aims have moral and ethical implications.

Regarding the first point about the entire created world, we can see the moral and ethical obligation of caring for creation. We are called to nurture the physical world, its creatures and its resources, rather than often exploiting them for our own greed and pleasure.[13] In this concern for nature, Teilhard is sometimes cited as a patron (saint) of ecology.[14]

Regarding the second part of his vision, Teilhard wanted to show how we can best nurture God's project by using all our time, talents, resources, and contacts to help God accomplish the divine plan of reconciling the world to himself in Christ (see 2 Cor 5:19). For Teilhard, one of our moral obligations is to develop an enriched and expanded consciousness that embraces more and more of reality in all its complexity.[15] Only then will we have developed a moral conscience that can love creation as God loves it.

According to John 3:16, *God loves creation as much as God loves his Son.*[16] For Teilhard, the universal Christ is the Divine Milieu in which all of us as well as all of creation live and move and enjoy a shared existence. Why does God love creation so much? Because it is an essential part of God's Son. Creation lives and moves and has its being in the Cosmic Christ. He is the Divine Milieu in which everything created lives.[17]

Appendix

Far from denying an original sin or a "fall," Teilhard wanted to give these powerful theological concepts a fresh cosmic reality. He wanted to revise our historical understanding of original sin and give it a new understanding in line with the universal Christ. For Teilhard, it is Christ who is at the center of history, not Adam and Eve. Christ always existed. He existed before history and will remain glorious after the end of history.

This basic idea for re-envisioning original sin was part of Teilhard's thinking from very early on. In a talk given in Paris in 1920, he said,

> "*If Christ is to be truly universal,* the Redemption, and hence the Fall, must extend to the whole universe. Original sin accordingly takes on a *cosmic nature* that tradition has always accorded to it, but which, in view of the new dimensions we recognize in our universe, obliges us radically to restate the historical representation of that sin and the too purely juridical way in which we commonly describe its being passed on."[18]

In a desire to explain more fully his approach to original sin, he presented his ideas in a paper he wrote in 1947 explicitly to be read and critiqued by qualified theologians.[19]

Regarding original sin, Teilhard was less focused on how sin entered the world and far more focused on safeguarding "the Christian understanding of Christ as Lord of the universe." At the same time, "he wants to be sure that man's place in the forward movement of the universe is not minimized."[20]

For Teilhard, the domain of original sin and all its effects cannot be assigned to any one place. It affects and infects the whole of time and space. He wrote, "If there is an original 'sin' in the world, it can only be and have been everywhere in it and always, from the earliest of the nebulae to be formed as the most distant."[21]

Teilhard never denied the existence of original sin and its effects. He expanded them. Also remember that the official doctrine of original sin states very clearly that it is not a sin in the usual sense of a consciously committed violation of God's commandments, but an inherited "condition" or "state." Teilhard asserted that *original sin is a general condition affecting not merely humans but the whole of creation from its origins* — even nebulae and stars. Original sin is transhistoric.

This new universal perspective on sin, Teilhard asserted, shows that "Christ's operation is quite truly co-extensive with the entire world." In this much broader definition of original sin, the universality of Christ's redemptive action and the evolution of the Cosmic Body of Christ (Christogenesis) are preserved. At the same time, salvation is revealed in its true breadth and depth. Everything God created is meant to enjoy salvation. Thus, all creation, not just humanity, is made whole and is meant to share in the fullness of life.[22]

Baptism and Original Sin

For most of Christian history, original sin has been closely connected with the sacrament of baptism. Teilhard dealt with that historical connection in a new way. He related baptism not merely to original sin and the expiation of sin on the cross, but more specifically to future positive personal and collective moral behavior.

We still live in what some have called a medieval religious context where what matters most for our salvation is reparation and expiation for that original sin of Adam and all the rest of humanity's sins. As traditional theologians understood it, Christ's main problem was how to rid that sinful stain in humanity. According to Christian tradition, Christ solved it by the supreme sacrifice of himself on the cross.

Christians have for centuries interpreted baptism almost exclusively in terms of purification from sin. Adults seeking baptism were taught that baptism removes not only original sin but also all their personal sins committed up to the moment of baptism. For infants with no personal sins to be purified, Christians were taught that baptism removes the stain of original sin. All this purification was accomplished by God's Son shedding his blood on the cross.

Without denying baptism's redemptive effects on original sin as well as on our past sins, Teilhard asserted that there was a broader and more forward-looking effect of baptism. An evolutionary effect. For him, ensuring the positive future of God's creation, not the removal of human sin, was Christ's main objective and challenge. If ensuring the positive future of God's creation was primary for Christ, it would require revising the main purpose of baptism from a *negative* emphasis (removal of original sin) to a *positive* one (conscious involvement in God's project). We have only to read the letters of St. Paul to see how the early church viewed the positive side of baptism as centrally important.[23]

The positive effects of baptism were most important to Teilhard because *by baptism we are formally and permanently connected to Christ*. In that connection, we are informed by Christ (in our being), conformed to him (in our thinking and acting), and transformed by him (by participating in Christogenesis). For Teilhard, that intimate connection to Christ has always been the most fundamental and important fact of our spiritual and physical life.

The Creator's more general presence in our lives—keeping us in existence—is "constantly backed by the particular presence of Christ."[24] We can, in fact, live always and everywhere without being separated from Jesus Christ. That is the most wonderful effect of baptism.

For Teilhard, the risen Christ is not an *intermediary* between the Creator and us, but, more properly, a *medium* (a *milieu* in French) uniting us to our Creator. For Teilhard, Christ is the Divine *Milieu*. To confirm the quality of this union of Jesus Christ and the Creator, Teilhard cited Jesus's statement to Philip, "Whoever has seen me has seen the Father" (John 14:9).[25]

Teilhard pointed out that even in traditional theology there have always been two distinct purposes for Christ's redemptive act on the cross: (1) expiation for sin; and (2) re-creation of the world in Christ, what we are calling God's project. "I came that they may have life, and have it abundantly" (John 10:10).

The same holds true when one looks at the two purposes of baptism. In the past, *expiation* of original sin was so strongly emphasized that baptism as a commitment to *re-creating the world in love* was seldom mentioned. Teilhard wanted to reprioritize those purposes.

Teilhard wanted to reverse the traditional purposes by placing the primary focus of baptism on the fact that, in baptism, we formally become members of Christ's Body working for the completion of God's project.[26] In this way, our moral *activities* can be used primarily to foster the completion of God's project. Yet, our efforts for Christ are also a way of showing gratitude to Christ for setting us free from sin. In this sense, it is also literally true that whatever the Christian does, it is to Christ that it is done. Not only to Christ, but also in Christ and with Christ.

Here is where Teilhard offered us new breadth and clarity to be "added to the mystery of the Cross"[27] as well as a forward thrust to living out the sacrament of baptism. In this way, with baptism, he established a connection between redemption and evolution.

Teilhard was proposing an understanding of baptism in which purification from sin becomes a subordinate element in the Christian's forward-looking commitment to participate actively in the cosmic divine act of raising up the world. In moral terms, *in baptism, the person in the presence of the faith community formally enlists in God's project and commits to doing the uniquely personal work only he or she can do toward its fulfillment.*

Similarly, Teilhard saw Christ applying the energy expended in his suffering on the cross more as driving the ascent of creation rather than as expiating sin. Clearing away our sins is merely a necessary but only a preliminary step in the larger project of building a new world. For example, if you plan to rebuild your home on your property, you must first tear down those parts of the old structure that you no longer want to keep (sin). This is an essential step. But it is not an end in itself. It is an essential step only because you are clearing the way to build a new home (God's project). Your major focus and where most of your energy and resources will be spent are not in the clearing away of the old, but rather in building the new structure. You invest most of your time, effort, and money on what you want to build (God's project).

Thus, Teilhard said, the blood of the cross is primarily "blood that circulates and vitalizes" the body of believers. Yes, Christ's blood is shed for sin, but only to clear away the old to inaugurate the new heavens and a new Earth. As Teilhard said, "The Lamb of God bears not only the sins of the world, but also the burden of its progress."[28]

It is to those who choose to be baptized into Christ's Body and wish to work on God's project that Jesus addresses the words, "Take my yoke upon you, and learn from me; for I am gentle and humble in heart, and you will find rest for your souls" (Matt 11:29). Jesus is welcoming the newly baptized to join him in the great work.

While baptism is seen primarily as an act that removes original sin and officially certifies one's membership in a parish's records, it is not much more than a one-time event. But if baptism is seen primarily as a commitment to working on God's project, then baptism has new meaning each day of one's life. For Teilhard, this reprioritization of the purpose of baptism could be used to energize people of all ages.

Notes

Preface

1. James Marsh is the British film and documentary director of many scientific-based movies, such as The Theory of Everything, the 2004 multi-award-winning biographical film about Stephen Hawking, the world-renowned theoretical physicist and cosmologist.

2. Michael Duffy, "Nine Questions for Klaus Schwab," TIME, January 23, 2017, 56.

1. An Emerging Moral Consciousness

1. The index in Robert L. Faricy's comprehensive work on Teilhard's thought, *Teilhard de Chardin's Theology of the Christian in the World* (New York: Sheed & Ward, 1967) proved most helpful in this search.

2. Billy Graham's website itemizes 127 messianic predictions found in the Hebrew Scriptures involving more than 3,000 biblical verses. See https://billygraham.org/decision-magazine/november.../the -promise-of-the-messiah/ (accessed January 9, 2019).

3. According to chapter 2 in the Book of Genesis, Adam and Eve were created by God directly as adults. What could it possibly mean to be "an adult" without years of experience, learning, and maturation?

4. Pierre Teilhard de Chardin, *Human Energy*, trans. J. M. Cohen (New York: Harper & Row, 1969), 109.

5. In chapter 8 of Paul's Letter to the Romans, Paul develops this theme of growth in the spirit. Those who lived in Christ no longer needed to follow an external law; they were guided by the inner law of the Spirit. Unfortunately, for most of the past millennium, the church did not encourage the faithful to develop a spirituality based on "listening to the Spirit."

6. Teilhard, *Human Energy*, 106.

2. Clarifications and Challenges

1. Ronald Cole-Turner, "Genetics and the Future of Humanity," in *Rediscovering Teilhard's Fire*, ed. Kathleen Duffy (Philadelphia: St. Joseph's University Press, 2010), 236.

2. For his simple explanation of these models, I am indebted to Edward Vacek, SJ, "An Evolving Christian Morality," in *From Teilhard to Omega*, ed. Ilia Delio (Maryknoll, NY: Orbis Books, 2014), 155–56.

3. Pierre Teilhard de Chardin, *Human Energy*, trans. J. M. Cohen (New York: Harper & Row, 1969), 106–7; Teilhard, *Activation of Energy*, trans. René Hague (New York: Harper & Row, 1970), 51–53, 71, 119.

4. Vacek, "An Evolving Christian Morality," 156.

5. Vacek, "An Evolving Christian Morality," 156.

6. Teilhard's evolutionary (natural) law will be discussed in greater detail in the following chapter.

7. Pierre Teilhard de Chardin, *Toward the Future*, trans. René Hague (New York: Harcourt Brace Jovanovich, 1974), 23. See also Teilhard, *The Future of Man*, trans. Norman Denny (New York: Harper & Row, 1964), 92.

8. See Acts 17:22–31; Rom 6:8–11; 8:22–23; 12:5; 14:7; Col 1:15–17: 2:19: 3:3; Gal 2:20; Eph 1:10, 23; 2:21.

9. See Louis M. Savary, *The Divine Milieu Explained* (New York: Paulist Press, 2007), esp. 27–39.

10. Teilhard, *Future of Man*, 93.

11. Teilhard, *Future of Man*, 92, 95.

12. See Louis M. Savary and Patricia H. Berne, *Teilhard de Chardin on Love* (New York: Paulist Press, 2017).

13. Teilhard, *Human Energy*, 32.

14. Teilhard, *Human Energy*, 31.

15. Teilhard, *Human Energy*, 29.

16. Teilhard, *Human Energy*, 150.

17. Teilhard, *Human Energy*, 30.

18. Teilhard, *Human Energy*, 44.

19. Teilhard, *Human Energy*, 137.

20. Pierre Teilhard de Chardin, *The Divine Milieu* (New York: Harper Colophon Books, 1960). For a fuller treatment with examples and spiritual exercises, see Louis M. Savary, *The Divine Milieu Explained*, 40–80.

3. Eight Basic Principles of Teilhard's Thought

1. Bruce Sanguin, *The Way of the Wind: The Path and Practice of Evolutionary Christian Mysticism* (Vancouver: Viriditas Press, 2015), 119.

2. Pierre Teilhard de Chardin, *Christianity and Evolution* (New York: Harcourt Brace Jovanovich, 1971), 185.

3. Teilhard's scientific phenomenology of evolution is the principal theme in his most famous book, *The Phenomenon of Man*, trans. Bernard Wall (New York: Harper & Row, 1959), or in a more recent translation *The Human Phenomenon*, trans. Sarah Appleton-Weber (Portland, OR: Sussex Academic Press, 2003).

4. Pierre Teilhard de Chardin, *Christianity and Evolution* (New York: Harcourt Brace Jovanovich, 1971), 238–39.

5. Robert L. Faricy, *Teilhard de Chardin's Theology of the Christian in the World* (New York: Sheed & Ward, 1967), 35–38.

6. See, e.g., Francis S. Collins, *The Language of God: A Scientist Presents Evidence for Belief* (New York: Free Press, 2006). K. Murakami, *The Divine Code of Life: Awaken Your Genius and Discover Hidden Talents* (Hillsboro, OR: Beyond Words Publications, 2006).

7. *National Geographic* dedicated its March 2015 issue to "The War on Science," 30–47. The article identified and described a sizable portion of Americans who continue to believe that evolution never happened, that climate change does not exist, and that the moon landing in 1969 was faked, a Hollywood stunt.

8. Teilhard, *The Human Phenomenon*, 152. An almost identical statement may be found in Teilhard, *Science and Christ*, trans. René Hague (New York: Harper & Row, 1968), 193.

9. Teilhard, *Phenomenon of Man*, 219. Teilhard also develops his ideas in a tightly written, short essay, "Degrees of Scientific Certainty in the Idea of Evolution," in *Science and Christ*, 192–96. See also T. Dobzhansky, "Nothing Makes Sense Except in the Light of Evolution," *American Biology Teacher* 35 (1973): 125–29.

10. Ilia Delio, *The Unbearable Wholeness of Being: God, Evolution, and the Power of Love* (Maryknoll, NY: Orbis Books, 2013), 19.

11. Pierre Teilhard de Chardin, *The Future of Man*, trans. Norman Denny (New York: Harper & Row, 1964), 54.

12. Pierre Teilhard de Chardin, *The Divine Milieu* (New York: Harper Colophon Books, 1960), 80–83.

13. To be precise, the adjective *evolutionary* is found at least once. *Gaudium et Spes,* The Pastoral Constitution on the Church in the Modern World, "Introductory Statement," no. 5.

14. Among the documents of Vatican II, The Pastoral Constitution on the Church in the Modern World (Latin title *Gaudium et Spes*) is perhaps the most forward-looking document produced by the Council. Much of the material in chapter 2, section 3, paragraph 62, of this document was most likely inspired by Teilhard, according to a footnote in Walter Abbott's *The Documents of Vatican II* (London: Chapman, 1966).

15. *Gaudium et Spes* 64.

16. Teilhard develops this theme in a lengthy article published in *Revue des Questions Scientifiques* in 1947. An English translation titled "The Formation of the Noosphere" may be found in *Future of Man,* 161–91.

17. Teilhard discusses the evolutionary law he discovered in its original two-stage version (Complexity-Consciousness) in many places, e.g., Pierre Teilhard de Chardin, *The Appearance of Man,* trans. J. M. Cohen (New York: Harper & Row, 1965), 236–37. The reader more deeply interested in this law may find three essays in Teilhard, *Activation of Energy,* trans. René Hague (New York: Harper & Row, 1970), of special interest: "The Atomism of Spirit," 21–58; "The Analysis of Life," 129–40; "On the Nature of the Phenomenon of Human Society," 165–68.

18. Although Teilhard never formulated this law in these four stages, the four stages are evident in his writings. See Louis M. Savary, "Expanding Teilhard's 'Complexity-Consciousness' Law," in *Teilhard Studies* 68 (Spring 2014).

19. Teilhard also talks about Attraction from a very different perspective, mentioned in an earlier section, as the *gravitational pull of the future.* (See *Future of Man,* 119.)

20. In several of his writings, Teilhard develops his insight that "Union differentiates." See *Future of Man,* 55–59 and *Human Energy,* trans. J. M. Cohen (New York: Harper & Row, 1969), 63, 69, 73, 104.

21. Teilhard discusses these terminology differences in *Future of Man,* 109.

22. Teilhard, *Science and Christ,* n77.

23. Teilhard, *Future of Man,* 56ff.

24. Teilhard, *Future of Man,* 111, 136.

Notes

25. See Faricy, *Teilhard de Chardin's Theology of the Christian in the World*, 63.

26. Liturgically, this focus on being with God in heaven is the objective of many of the prescribed prayers at daily Mass, and almost universally the explicit request found in the designated priestly prayers after communion.

27. Teilhard, *Christianity and Evolution*, 28, 31–34, 179; *The Divine Milieu*, 62–64, 85.

28. Teilhard, *Christianity and Evolution*, 160; *The Divine Milieu*, 64.

29. Nano is short for nanometer. There are 1,000,000,000 (a billion) nanometers in one meter.

30. See David Szondy, "Super-Resolved Fluorescence Microscopy Pioneers Awarded 2014 Nobel Prize in Chemistry," New Atlas, October 10, 2014, www.gizmag.com/nobel-nanomicroscopy/34182/.

31. Teilhard discusses the relationship between the Divine Milieu and the Cosmic Christ in part 3 of his *The Divine Milieu*, 112–55. For him, these are merely two names to describe the same reality.

32. According to Paul in Romans 8, the Spirit is helping us mature and grow in spirit, enabling us to "walk according to the Spirit" and follow the inner "law of the Spirit." This inner law of the Spirit, Teilhard might say, is the law of Attraction-Connection-Complexity-Consciousness.

33. Paul is also quite aware of the immaturity of some of his new converts. See 1 Cor 3:1–9.

34. This brief quotation comes from Luther's "Defense of All the Articles." At one point in this work from 1521, Luther contends with those who say that after baptism, no sin remains in the Christian. Luther argues from Scripture that the Christian's sins are forgiven through Christ, but also that there remains in the Christian an ongoing battle against sin. And this battle is not fought in vain. See http://www.godrules.net/library/luther/NEW1luther_c4.htm (accessed January 10, 2019).

35. Pierre Teilhard de Chardin, *Hymn of the Universe*, trans. J. M. Cohen (New York: Harper & Row, 1969), 132–33.

36. Teilhard, *Hymn of the Universe*, 114.

37. Teilhard, *Hymn of the Universe*, 115.

38. Teilhard, *Hymn of the Universe*, 131–32.

39. Teilhard, *Future of Man*, 207–8: "One may say that until the coming of Man, it was natural selection that set the course of morphogenesis and cerebration, but that after Man it is the power of invention that begins to grasp the evolutionary reins."

40. Teilhard, *The Divine Milieu*, 60–82; *Hymn of the Universe*, 92–93.

41. Edward Vacek, "An Evolving Christian Morality," in *From Teilhard to Omega*, ed. Ilia Delio (Maryknoll, NY: Orbis Books, 2014), 157.

42. In his chapter on ethics, "An Evolving Christian Morality," Vacek cites several references to Teilhard's statements on the Christogenesis theme: *Activation of Energy*, 279; *Science and Christ*, 17; *Christianity and Evolution*, 71–75, 177–79; *The Divine Milieu*, 61–62, 138–40; *The Future of Man*, 22.

43. Even in the Hebrew Scriptures, the primary commandment is about love. The only thing God asks of us is love. "Thou shall love the Lord thy God with thy whole mind, soul and strength. And you are to love your neighbor as yourself." Nothing is mentioned in that commandment about fear, worship, sacrifice, etc. Just a response of love.

44. See Teilhard, *Science and Christ*, 68.

45. Teilhard, *Science and Christ*, 167–71.

46. Teilhard, *Human Energy*, 32.

47. John F. Haught, *Deeper than Darwin* (Cambridge, MA: Westview, 2003), 174.

48. Teilhard, *Science and Christ*, 57.

49. In Paul's passage on love, he lists thirteen qualities of love. See 1 Cor 13:4–8.

50. The notion of love as energy is most fully developed in Louis M. Savary and Patricia H. Berne, *Teilhard de Chardin on Love* (Mahwah, NJ: Paulist, 2017).

51. *Spiritual Exercises of St. Ignatius Loyola*, no. 230. Teilhard discusses this idea of the centrality of action in *Science and Christ*, 174–86.

52. English translations miss the point entirely by translating *agape* and *philia*, two very different levels of love, equally as "love."

53. Teilhard, *Science and Christ*, 175.

54. See Teilhard, *Science and Christ*, 167–73: "To cooperate in total cosmic evolution is the only deliberate act that can adequately express our devotion to an evolutive and universal Christ," 169.

55. Teilhard, *Science and Christ*, 172.

56. "Jesus said to him, 'I am the way, and the truth, and the life'" (John 14:6).

57. Many suggestions for developing and maintaining loving relationships may be found in Savary and Berne, *Teilhard de Chardin on Love*.

58. Thomas Merton, *New Seeds of Contemplation* (New York: New Directions, 1961), 76.

59. Teilhard, *Future of Man*, 119.

60. Ilia Delio, "Evolution and the Rise of the Secular God," in *From Teilhard to Omega: Co-creating an Unfinished Universe*, ed. Ilia Delio (Maryknoll, NY: Orbis Books, 2014), 49.

61. Teilhard, *Future of Man*, 119.

62. Teilhard, *Christianity and Evolution*, 182, 226, 239.

63. This all-embracing love of God permeating all elements of ____ creation is one major theme of Teilhard's *The Divine Milieu*. "God is as pervasive and perceptible as the atmosphere in which we are bathed. He encompasses us on all sides, like the world itself. What prevents you, then, from enfolding him in your arms? Only one thing: your inability to *see* him." *Divine Milieu*, 46. The rest of that book presents Teilhard teaching us *how to see*.

64. Teilhard, *Science and Christ*, 52. *Divine Milieu*, 114. For Teilhard, *cosmogenesis* and *Christogenesis* refer essentially to the same maturation process, one viewed from a scientific perspective, the other from a theological perspective.

65. Teilhard's most important essay on the noosphere, written in 1947, is "The Formation of the Noosphere," in *Future of Man*, 161–91.

66. Teilhard, *Future of Man*, 176–81.

67. Teilhard, *Future of Man*, 177.

68. Peter Russell, *The Global Brain Awakens: Our Next Evolutionary Leap*. The third or fourth edition was published by Element Books, 2000. Amazon offers only used copies of the 1995 hardback edition. The earliest edition in 1982 was published in England as *The Awakening Earth*.

69. Teilhard, *Future of Man*, 178.

70. Teilhard, *Future of Man*, 181–87.

71. Teilhard, *Future of Man*, 178.

72. Teilhard, *Science and Christianity*, 77.

73. Teilhard, *Christianity and Evolution*, 227. *Toward the Future*, trans. René Hague (New York: Harcourt Brace Jovanovich, 1974), 131–32. For a development of his metaphysics of *unire*, see *Toward the Future*, 192–98. German Jesuit theologian Karl Rahner (1904–84) faced the same problem as Teilhard but resolved it differently. A comparison of their metaphysical approaches is beyond the scope of this book.

74. See, e.g., 1 Cor 13:4–8; Matt 25:34–40; and Jesus's Sermon on the Mount in Matt 5–7.

75. Cf. Deut 6:5 and note that this is reemphasized in all Synoptic Gospels. See Matt 22:37; Mark 12:30–31.

76. Delio, *From Teilhard to Omega*, 189.

77. Teilhard scholar Ursula King developed this important concept of Teilhard in her essay, "The Zest for Life: A Contemporary Exploration of a Generative Theme in Teilhard's Work" in Delio, *From Teilhard to Omega*, 184–202.

78. Teilhard, *Christianity and Evolution*, 228.

79. Teilhard, *Christianity and Evolution*, 238–39.

80. Teilhard, *Christianity and Evolution*, 183–86.

81. Teilhard, *Future of Man*, 110–14.

82. Teilhard, *Future of Man*, 117–24.

83. Teilhard, *Future of Man*, 120.

84. Teilhard, *Future of Man*, 122–23.

4. Eleven Principles of Teilhard's Ethics

1. "Do not be conformed to this world, but be transformed by the renewing of your minds, so that you may discern what is the will of God—what is good and acceptable and perfect" (Rom 12:2). In the original Greek, Paul is calling for a metamorphosis of one's self to a higher state by a total transformation of one's way of thinking.

2. Although these principles are derived from Teilhard's Roman Catholic theological perspective and his vision of Christogenesis, I am sure he would prefer to see them formulated as they are here, in ways acceptable to all humans (cosmogenesis). However, in each case, I present their development from Teilhard's own Christian scriptural and theological perspective.

3. For Teilhard, the work of God's project cannot move forward in full strength without the participation of the different world faiths.

Notes

See his essay "The Spirit of the Earth," in *Human Energy*, trans. J. M. Cohen (New York: Harper & Row, 1969), 19–47. See also Ursula King, "Teilhard's Cosmic Spirituality," in *Rediscovering Teilhard's Fire*, ed. Kathleen Duffy (Philadelphia: Saint Joseph's University Press, 2010), 19. This is not a new notion. See Jer 31:33–34.

4. Teilhard identified this as the law of Attraction-Connection-Complexity-Consciousness. *Christianity and Evolution* (New York: Harcourt Brace Jovanovich, 1971), 29.

5. St. Paul expands on this idea of each one in the community, as members of Christ's Body, having different qualifications and different works to perform (see 1 Cor 12:18–20). We suffer together and rejoice together (see 1 Cor 12:26). Each person has unique gifts, and no one has every gift (see 1 Cor 12:28–31). Everyone is graced with the gifts of faith, hope, and love.

6. Among the gifts given to everyone, love is the greatest. "It bears all things, believes all things, hopes all things, endures all things. Love never ends" (1 Cor 13:7–8).

7. St. Paul's opinion is clear regarding those who are not using their gifts to nurture the community (2 Thess 3:10–13).

8. St. Paul treats his immature followers gently but firmly. See 1 Cor 3:1–9.

9. *Teilhard de Chardin: Pilgrim of the Future*, ed. N. Braybrooke (New York: Libra Books, 1964), 23–26.

10. Teilhard describes these two purposes as the "Cross of Expiation" and the "Cross of Evolution" in *Christianity and Evolution*, 216–19. He notes that the institutional church in its liturgy and catechesis sometimes presents only the Cross of Expiation. St. Paul certainly saw both. See next note.

11. St. Paul recognizes and actively participates in Christ's second, and perhaps larger, purpose of suffering on the cross, when he writes to his community, "I am now rejoicing in my sufferings for your sake, and in my flesh *I am completing what is lacking in Christ's afflictions for the sake of his body*, that is, the church" (Col 1:24, emphasis added). Bringing his Cosmic Body to maturity is something to which all of us can contribute (see Col 1:28–29 and Col 2:6–7).

12. See Louis M. Savary and Patricia H. Berne, *Teilhard de Chardin: Seven Stages of Suffering; A Spiritual Path for Transformation* (Mahwah, NJ: Paulist Press, 2015), for ways to apply the energy you expend in suffering.

13. Louis M. Savary and Patricia H. Berne, *Why Did God Make Me? Finding Your Life's Purpose; Discernment in an Evolutionary World* (Mahwah, NJ: Paulist Press, 2014). It provides a discernment process based on the evolutionary law of Attraction-Connection-Complexity-Consciousness.

14. Teilhard, *Christianity and Evolution*, 221–22, 238–39.

15. As I recall, the book by P. D. Ouspensky was either *The Fourth Way* or *The Psychology of Man's Possible Evolution*.

16. Teilhard, *Christianity and Evolution*, 92.

17. Teilhard, *Christianity and Evolution*, 92.

18. Pierre Teilhard de Chardin, *The Divine Milieu* (New York: Harper Colophon Books, 1960), 60–61.

19. Nicholas Kristof, "Making America Meaner," *New York Times*, 2016, reprinted in *Tampa Bay Times*, August 21, 2016, 4P.

20. Justin Worland, "Destiny Watford: Fighting to Breathe," *TIME*, June 13, 2016, 49.

21. Worland, "Destiny Watford," 49.

22. I remember talking to a religious sister who taught a second-grade class, in which over a third of the students did not speak English. I asked her how she coped. With a snicker and a smile, she replied, "I teach a lot of arithmetic."

23. Teilhard, *Science and Christ*, trans. René Hague (New York: Harper & Row, 1968), 180.

24. Teilhard, *Science and Christ*, 68.

25. Teilhard, *Science and Christ*, 67–68.

26. Francis S. Collins, *The Language of God: A Scientist Presents Evidence for Belief* (New York: Free Press, 2006).

27. As many saints discovered, some of the strongest temptations to sin occur during prayer time. Jesus himself discovered this fact in his temptations in the desert (see Matt 4:1–11; Mark 1:12–13; Luke 4:1–13).

28. This is not to deny the importance of prayer, but to situate it in the context of Christogenesis, the work of building the Body of Christ. Juan Luis Segundo points out that the only scriptural reference to the value of contemplation over action is the scene where Mary of Bethany sits contemplatively at the feet of Jesus, while Martha is busy with kitchen duties. If you read the Sermon on the Mount, Jesus's words are a call to action. When Jesus encourages his disciples to pray and fast, it is so they can carry out more effectively their mission of healing. The

Lord's Prayer itself is future oriented. It is a call to action, to help make evident on Earth the presence of the kingdom of God. "Thy kingdom come. Thy will be done on Earth." See Juan Luis Segundo, *The Christ of the Ignatian Exercises* (Maryknoll, NY: Orbis Books, 1987).

29. Teilhard, *Human Energy*, 126.

30. Teilhard, *Human Energy*, 127. (Teilhard's emphasis).

31. Dr. Henderson's work was described in the *Tampa Bay Times*, August 28, 2016, 4A.

32. Teilhard, *The Divine Milieu*, 72.

33. Teilhard, *The Divine Milieu*, 72.

34. See Teilhard, *The Divine Milieu*, 66. Teilhard is merely echoing St. Paul: see Col 3:17, 23.

35. "Albert Einstein and the Atomic Bomb," accessed January 14, 2019, http://www.doug-long.com/einstein.htm.

36. In this regard, he develops three concepts: "detachment" (70–73), "diminishment" (74ff.), and "death" (81–81, 88–89).

37. Teilhard, *The Divine Milieu*, 70.

38. Teilhard called this hyphenated life "religious schizophrenia." *Christianity and Evolution*, 213.

39. Teilhard, *Science and Christ*, 59–60.

40. Teilhard, *Christianity and Evolution*, 227.

41. Teilhard, *Christianity and Evolution*, 49.

42. *Habitat for Humanity Seattle-King County*, accessed January 14, 2019, https://www.habitatskc.org/get-involved/donate/.

43. Victoria Richards, "Tampa Honda Helps a Single Mother Celebrate the Purchase of Her New Home," *Habitat for Humanity of Hillsborough County, Florida*, May 30, 2016, accessed January 14, 2019, https://www.habitathillsborough.org/tampa-honda-provides-keys-pate-family/.

44. Unknown author, "Breakfast at McDonalds," in *Fe-mails: Ecelebrating Women One Click at a Time*, ed. Millicent Perry (New York: iUniverse, 2005), 6–7.

45. Quoted in Paula Spencer Scott, "Throw Kindness Around Like Confetti: It's the Little Things We Do That Make All the Difference," *Parade*, January 1, 2017, 8–10.

46. Teilhard, *The Future of Man*, trans. Norman Denny (New York: Harper & Row, 1964), 142.

47. Teilhard, *Future of Man*, 142.

48. "I came that they may have life, and have it abundantly" (John 10:10).

49. See Rom 8:20–23.

50. Teilhard develops this point at length in *Christianity and Evolution*, 86–90.

51. Teilhard, *Christianity and Evolution*, 92.

52. The Greek word used in Gen 1:28 is *arksete*, from the verb *arkseuo*, which means "to lead or command, to be at the head of, to be first, to be a model for the rest." It is a call to humanity's leadership: to demonstrate courage, forethought, skill, observation, and good judgment in dealing with Earth's creatures and resources.

53. Aryn Baker, "Saran Kaba Jones: Quenching a Nation's Thirst," *TIME*, June 13, 2016, 45.

54. Video adapted from KUAC-TV and the Geophysical Institute at the University of Alaska, Fairbanks. See www.pbslearningmedia.org.

55. News 8 WKBT in LaCrosse, Wisconsin, recognizes area students who are going above and beyond to give back in their communities by volunteering. See www.News8000.com.

56. Robert Faricy, *Teilhard de Chardin's Theology of the Christian in the World* (New York: Sheed & Ward, 1967), 21–22.

57. Matthew Kelly, ed., *Beautiful Mercy: Experiencing God's Unconditional Love So We Can Share It with Others* (Erlanger, KY: Dynamic Catholic Institute, 2015), 5.

58. Kelly, *Beautiful Mercy*, 5–6.

59. Maya Wei-Haas, "The True Story of 'Hidden Figures,' the Forgotten Women Who Helped Win the Space Race," *Smithsonian Magazine*, September 8, 2016. Their story was also put into a movie called *Hidden Figures*.

60. Wei-Haas, "The True Story of 'Hidden Figures.'"

61. Maura Rhodes, "Sunday with Sally Field," *Parade*, March 13, 2016, 9.

62. Nikhil Kumar, "Umesh Sachdev: Digital Translator," *TIME*, July 13, 2016, 45.

63. Pope John Paul II, Prayer Vigil at World Youth Day, August 19, 2000.

64. Josh Sandburn, "The City Where High School Grads Go to College for Free," *TIME Magazine*, July 11–18, 2016, 80.

65. "Hope Alive," *Red Cloud Indian School Newsletter*, Summer 2016, vol. 8, issue 1.

66. Her story was told by David Brooks, "A Moral Bucket List," *New York Times Sunday Review*, April 11, 2015.

67. T. Berry Brazelton and Stanley I. Greenspan, "Why Children Need Nurturing Relationships, Grades PreK–K, 1–2." See http://www.scholastic.com/teachers/article/professional-development-why-children-need-ongoing-nurturing-relationships (accessed January 15, 2019).

68. Alice Park, "Life, the Remix," *TIME Magazine*, July 4, 2016, 42–48. By the way, CRISPR stands for Clustered Regularly Interspaced Short Palindromic Repeats.

69. Park, "Life, the Remix," 45.

70. Jerome R. Stockfisch, "Tampa Dad's PikMyKid App Streamlines Fetching Kids at School," *Tampa Bay Times*, Sunday, June 26, 2016, D1.

71. Tim Muldoon, "Keeping Young People Connected," *Extension Magazine*, Fall 2013, 16.

72. This is the first sentence of "The Principle and Foundation" in St. Ignatius Loyola's decision-making discernment process called *The Spiritual Exercises*.

73. Teilhard called the scope of our talents and action "a field for our effort." See *Christianity and Evolution*, 226.

74. Teilhard, *Christianity and Evolution*, 221–23.

75. Brooks, "A Moral Bucket List."

76. Faricy, *Teilhard de Chardin's Theology of the Christian in the World*, 147–48. Teilhard's ideas about original sin, however, are what got him in trouble with the church. Teilhard's explanation of original sin is discussed in the appendix.

77. Faricy, *Teilhard de Chardin's Theology of the Christian in the World*, 147.

78. Teilhard, *Science and Christ*, 80n.

79. Teilhard, *Christianity and Evolution*, 146.

80. Teilhard values Jesus's statement that it is necessary for scandals (evils) to occur (see Matt 18:17). He refers to it many times when he discusses the inevitability of evils occurring in an evolving universe.

81. Sara Dinatale, "A Home to Help the Needy Find One," in *Tampa Bay Times*, April 9, 2016, B1 and B6.

82. See, e.g., Rom 8:12–17 and 12:10–17.

83. Thankfully, Catholic social teaching since Vatican II has become very explicit about social sin, especially during the pontificate of Pope John Paul II (1978–2005). See John Paul II, *Reconciliatio et Paenitentia* (1984), no. 2, and Pontifical Council for Justice and Peace, *Compendium of the Social Doctrine of the Church* (Washington, DC: U.S. Conference of Catholic Bishops, 2005), nos. 115–19.

84. See *Christianity and Evolution*, 144–45, where Teilhard describes the current shift in ethics from "individual rights" to "obligations that are collective and social in nature."

85. Although Teilhard does not use the phrase *social sin* in his writings, it is clear from his description of the noosphere that, for the most part, people think and act collectively, for good and ill. See "The Formation of the Noosphere," in *Future of Man*, 161–91. Here, he says, "With every day that passes it becomes a little more impossible for us to act or think otherwise than collectively," 177.

86. Charles E. Curran, "Facing Up to Privilege Requires Conversion: An Essay," in *National Catholic Reporter*, June 17–30, 2016, 16–17.

87. Rachel L. Swarns, "Georgetown University Plans Steps to Atone for Slave Past," *New York Times*, September 1, 2016, https://www.nytimes.com/2016/09/02/us/slaves-georgetown-university.html.

88. Swarns, "Georgetown University Plans Steps to Atone for Slave Past."

89. E.g., Pope John Paul II emphasizes that every situation of social sin is "the result of the accumulation and concentration of many personal sins." See John Paul II, *Reconciliatio et Paenitentia* (1984), no. 16, as well as Pope John Paul II, *Sollicitudo Rei Socialis* (On Social Concern) (1987), nos. 36, 65.

90. *Christianity and Evolution*, 138. Teilhard implies that Rome was afraid that he was "addressing the great mass of believers and nonbelievers, in an attempt to open up for them a boundlessly enlarged field of worship."

91. In a rather long paper, "How I Believe," Teilhard set out some of his personal theological and ethical principles. *Christianity and Evolution*, 96–132.

92. The story of Teilhard's informal trial in Rome in 1948 is told in detail in Mary Lucas and Ellen Lucas, *Teilhard: A Biography* (London: Collins, 1977), 248–57.

93. This defensive position was exemplified in an obligatory oath against modernism (a theological position that Pope Pius X called "a synthesis of all heresies"), demanded of all clergy and teachers to be sworn to in public, ordered by Pope Pius X in 1910. One of its demands was to believe that the world was created exactly as described in the opening chapters of Genesis. The requirement to take this oath was finally canceled by Pope Paul VI in 1967.

94. "Dear Abby," *Tampa Bay Times*, Saturday, July 9, 2016, 1F. Dear Abby is written by Abigail Van Buren, also known as Jeanne Phillips. See www.dearabby.com.

95. Teilhard describes the elements of this stage in his essay, "Christianity and Evolution: Suggestions for a New Theology," *Christianity and Evolution*, 173–86.

96. Teilhard, "Christianity and Evolution," 186.

97. Eckhart Tolle, *A New Earth: Awakening to Your Life's Purpose*, 10th anniv. ed. (New York: Penguin Books, 2016), xv.

98. Pierre Teilhard de Chardin, *Hymn of the Universe*, trans. J. M. Cohen (New York: Harper & Row, 1969), 19–21.

99. Teilhard, *Science and Christ*, 169.

100. Teilhard develops this level of Christogenesis-consciousness in his "Mass on the World," *Hymn of the Universe*, 29–32, and in part 3 of *The Divine Milieu*, 112–49.

101. Teilhard, *Science and Christ*, 169.

102. Teilhard, *The Divine Milieu*, 121–28.

103. See Joel R. Primack and Nancy Ellen Abrams, *The View from the Center of the Universe: Discovering Our Extraordinary Place in the Cosmos* (New York: Riverhead Books, 2007), for more explanation of this fascinating perspective.

104. This is the intent of Pope Francis encyclical *Laudato Sí: On Care for Our Common Home*.

105. Bruce Sanguin, *The Way of the Wind: The Path and Practice of Evolutionary Christian Mysticism* (Vancouver: Viriditas Press, 2015), 135.

Appendix: Teilhard on Original Sin and Baptism

1. The term *original sin* is not found in Scripture. It was first alluded to in the second century by Irenaeus. See appropriate scholarly references on "original sin" in Wikipedia.

2. Much scientific evidence from geological and anthropological data showed the prevalence of sickness, suffering, and death among living creatures long before humans appeared on the planet. Teilhard was faced with these facts when he looked at the Garden of Eden story.

3. The Oath against Modernism was promulgated in *Sacrorum Antistitum*, a personal document (or *motu proprio*) signed by Pius X in 1910.

4. The swearing of the oath was compulsory for all Catholic bishops, priests, and theology teachers, until its abolition by Pope Paul VI in 1967.

5. Tradition assures us that concupiscence is not a sin in itself, but rather "the tinder for sin," that is, it may be likened to a flammable substance (tinder wood) that is easily ignited by a spark.

6. Teilhard observes that such an Adam would be "most ill-adapted to bearing in himself the complete responsibilities of our race." *Christianity and Evolution* (New York: Harcourt Brace Jovanovich, 1969), 46.

7. Teilhard uses "evil" in its classical definition as a *deprivation of being or lack of good*, not merely as a conscious violation of the moral law.

8. Since the evolutionary process and the "laws of becoming" are "modalities rigorously imposed on God's action, then we can begin to see that the *existence of evil* might very well also be a *strictly inevitable* concomitant of an evolving creation. '*Necesse est ut adveniant scandala.*'" ("For it is necessary that trials come," see Matt 18:7). *Christianity and Evolution*, 33.

9. Even in Teilhard's day, scriptural scholars were interpreting the first chapters of Genesis not as a literal or visual depiction of *human history*, but rather as insights into ancient understandings of *human nature*. St. Augustine warned preachers in the early church that the Creation stories in Genesis should be interpreted symbolically and figuratively rather than taken literally.

10. Teilhard, *Christianity and Evolution*, 80.

11. It is illuminating to note that in his letters, Paul refers to Jesus of Nazareth only a handful of times, whereas he refers to "Jesus Christ" or "Christ Jesus" well over 150 times. This highlights Paul's primary concern about the future of Christ's universal Body.

12. Most of Teilhard's essays that treat original sin may be found in one volume of his collected writings, *Christianity and Evolution*.

13. Pope Francis developed this theme in his 2015 encyclical *Laudato Si: On Care for Our Common Home*.

14. See Thomas Berry, *The Great Work: Our Way into the Future* (New York: Bell Tower, 1999).

15. A clear example of an expanded consciousness that has occurred during the past century is humanity's concern for the whole world. Today, we are showing ecological concern for the planet as a whole—fishing rights, oil drilling rights, reducing the use of fossil fuels, developing renewable sources of energy. All these are signs of an expanding human consciousness.

16. The text in John 3:16 may be colloquially translated, "God loved the cosmos so much that he gave it the gift of his only Son." God could have bestowed on creation some lesser gift, but God gifted it with the fullness of divinity in Christ. We can say that *God loves creation as much as God loves his Son, since in him all creation has become—has always been—one Cosmic Being, the Son.*

17. This is the conclusion of Teilhard's famous spirituality book *The Divine Milieu*.

18. Teilhard, "Note on the Universal Christ," reprinted in *Science and Christ* (New York: Harper & Row, 1965), 16.

19. Teilhard, "Reflections on Original Sin." His paper may be found in the book *Christianity and Evolution*, 187–98.

20. Robert L. Faricy, *Teilhard de Chardin's Theology of the Christian in the World* (New York: Sheed & Ward, 1967), 153–54.

21. Faricy, *Teilhard de Chardin's Theology of the Christian in the World*, 190. In a 1920 essay, "The Fall, Redemption and Geocentricism," Teilhard writes, "The *spirit* of the Bible and the Church is perfectly clear: the *whole* world has been corrupted by the Fall and the *whole* of everything has been redeemed." *Christianity and Evolution*, 39 (Teilhard's emphasis).

22. "I came that they may have life, and have it abundantly" (John 10:10). The primary and ultimate purpose for Jesus's life was *to bring the fullness of life to creation.*

23. For Paul, baptism not only removes sin, but it enables you to do the work "to which indeed you were called in the one body" (Col 3:12–15). For other benefits of baptism that help us share in building the Body of Christ, see, e.g., 1 Cor 12—13; 2 Cor 5; Gal 3—5; Eph 2—4; Phil 2.

24. See Teilhard, *Christianity and Evolution,* 18.

25. Teilhard, *Christianity and Evolution,* 20.

26. Teilhard, *Christianity and Evolution,* 146. To Teilhard, it was clear that Augustine held the same positive primacy for baptism. For Augustine, *the new heavens and a new Earth* (the consummation of creation in God) were the fruit and the price of the sacrifice of the cross. See Teilhard, *Christianity and Evolution,* 145.

27. Teilhard, *Christianity and Evolution,* 85.

28. Teilhard, *Christianity and Evolution,* 146.

Bibliography

Teilhard Books

Pierre Teilhard de Chardin. *Activation of Energy*. Translated by René Hague. New York: Harper & Row, 1970.

————. *The Appearance of Man*. Translated by J. M. Cohen. New York: Harper & Row, 1965.

————. *Christianity and Evolution*. New York: Harcourt Brace Jovanovich, 1971.

————. *The Divine Milieu*. New York: Harper Colophon Books, 1960.

————. *The Future of Man*. Translated by Norman Denny. New York: Harper & Row, 1964.

————. *Human Energy*. Translated by J. M. Cohen. New York: Harper & Row, 1969.

————. *Hymn of the Universe*. New York: Harper & Row, 1965.

————. *The Phenomenon of Man*. Translated by Bernard Wall. New York: Harper & Row, 1959. Also published as *The Human Phenomenon*. Translated by Sarah Appleton-Weber. Portland, OR: Sussex Academic Press, 2003.

————. *Science and Christ*. Translated by René Hague. New York: Harper & Row, 1968.

INDEX

Index

113, 115; Christianity, 31;
cooperation with God, 56–57;
definition of term, 10;
development, 137; evolution,
5, 13, 31; God's project,
72, 75; involvement, 73;
love, 52–53, 64; medicine,
29; models, 11–13; the
noosphere, 60; passivities,
19; principles, 2, 67–72;
privacy, 29; responsibilties,
91, 116; Teilhard's thought, 2;
traditional, 76, 91; union, 64.
See also Morality; Principles
evil, 121–22, 125, 153–54, 176n5,
176n8
Evolution: Catholics in America,
80; and Christianity, 5, 31,
127; of church, 27–28, 81, 152;
Consciousness, 35; constant,
30; continuity,
15–16; and creation, 23;
Darwin, 23–24; ethics, 5, 13,
31; evidence, 24, 29–30;
and evil, 121, 176n8; fast,
28; genome, 24–25; God's
project, 13–14, 26, 58, 72;
good works, 48; *Homo sapiens*,
155; humanity, 16, 43, 58;
imagination, 85; laws, 32;
Level Five, 143; levels of
existence, 25–26; living, 32;
love, 52, 57; messy, 26; moral
directive, 76; morality, 4,
8, 76, 147–48; natural, 30–
31; natural law model, 13;
noosphere, 58; nurturing, 101,
108; and original sin, 152,
154–55; Paul, 114; process, 25;
progress, 28–29; purpose, 25;
questions, 24–25; random, 32;
and redemption, 160; rejected

by church, 152; resources,
108; science, 24, 26; slow, 27;
spirituality, 21–22; trial and
error, 26–27; universal, 25;
using the four-stage law, 36–37;
Vatican II, 28; war on science,
163n7. *See also* Creation;
God's project
Expiation, 158, 159, 160, 169n10

Facebook, 64
Faith, 3
Faricy, Robert, 24, 102, 120
FedEx, 91
Field, Sally, 106
Four-stage law, 36–37. *See also*
Law of Attraction-Connection-
Complexity-Consciousness
Fragments, 15
Francis, Pope, 98–99, 143
Francis of Assisi, 44
Free zones, 126

Galilei, Galileo, 23
Gandhi, Mahatma, 136
Gaudium et Spes, 28
Genesis, Book of, 23, 25, 50, 151,
153, 176n9
Gentiles, 4–5
Georgetown University, 134
Global mentality, 59
God: consciousness, 35;
cooperation with humans, 37,
39–40, 42, 43–44, 45, 56–57;
Creator, 29, 30, 46, 55,
57–58, 96–97, 159, 167n63;
development, 70; and Earth,
97; emptying, 55–56;
forgiveness, 69–70;
God's project, 58, 68–69;
immutability, 47; and Jesus
Christ, 159; love, 46–47, 49,

183

Morality: action, 69; activities
and passivities, 18, 19; and
baptism, 160; challenges, 1–2;
consciousness, 2, 3–4, 15,
137–45, 142–44; contrasts,
6–8; creaturely activity,
39; definition of term, 10;
development, 70, 73–74, 115,
116, 118, 137–45; evolution,
4, 8, 76, 147–48; and God, 11;
God's project, 26, 69; levels,
137–45; love, 64; the
noosphere, 60; revolution, 44;
safe, 88; Teilhard's thought
on, 1; traditional, 6–8, 38,
72–73, 88–89, 148. *See also*
Consciousness;
Ethics; Principles
Moral theology, 6–7, 73
Moses, 95
Musk, Elon, 81, 84

Nanoscopy, 40
NASA, 105
Nations, 59
Neanderthals, 155
Needs, 52–53
New commandment, the 54
Newman, Henry, 3
Nicodemus, 47, 96–97
Noosphere, 57–60

Obedience or duty stage, 138–39
Old covenant, 130
*Ordinary People Change the
World*, 104

Paradox, 55–56
Passivities, 17–19
Pastoral Constitution on the
Church in the Modern World,
164n14

Pate, Pricilla, 92, 93
Paul, Apostle, 4, 14–15, 41, 48,
113–15, 130, 154, 161n5,
165n32, 168n1, 169n5, 169n11
Perfection, 30–31, 57
Perkins, Francis, 109–10,
115–16
Personal moral conscience stage,
140–41
Peter, Apostle, 50
Pill, the, 116–18
Pincus, Gregory, 116, 117
Pius X, Pope, 152
Positive difference, 76, 77, 80, 83,
84
prayer, 69, 82, 170n28
Principles: basic, 22, 72; ethical,
2, 67–72; ethical principle 1,
72–76; ethical principle 2, 76–
83; ethical principle 3, 83–91;
ethical principle 4, 91–101;
ethical principle 5, 101–8;
ethical principle 6, 108–13;
ethical principle 7, 113–20;
ethical principle 8, 120–30;
ethical principle 9, 130–36;
ethical principle 10, 137–45;
ethical principle 11,
145–49; God, 11; humanity,
68; Level Four, 140; principle
of Teilhard's thought 1,
23–31; principle of Teilhard's
thought 2, 32–37; principle of
Teilhard's thought 3,
38–42, principle of Teilhard's
thought 4, 42–46; principle of
Teilhard's thought 5,
46–53; principle of Teilhard's
thought 6, 53–57; principle of
Teilhard's thought 7, 57–61,
principle of Teilhard's
thought 8, 61–65; sin, 69

Index

Purpose, 25, 38–39, 54, 57–58, 65, 75–76, 77, 145

Racism, 133–34
Reason, 3
Red Cloud Indian School, 109
Religion: true function, 16
Resources, 108, 109, 110, 111–12
Responsibility, 31, 80, 91–92, 96, 116, 145, 156
Reward and punishment stage, 137–38
Roberts, Bruce, 129
Rock, John, 116–18
Roman Catholics in America, 79–80
Roosevelt, Franklin, 87, 110, 116
Rules, 8–9, 10, 12, 71
Russell, Peter, 59

Sachdev, Umesh, 107
Sacred, 90
Salvation, 53–54, 60, 97, 158
Sarogi, Ravi, 107
Science, 6, 24, 26, 89, 127, 128, 163n7
Scripture, 62, 166n43
Segundo, Juan Luis, 170n28
Self-centeredness, 135
Self-emptying, 55–56
Self-evolution, 118
Self-expression, 50
Sheed, Frank, 45
Sheed & Ward, 45
Shetterly, Margot Lee, 105–6
Silencing of Teilhard, 151. *See also* Censorship of Teilhard
Sin: and baptism, 158, 165n34;

of commission, 124; cosmic, 157; disunity, 122–23; ethical principles, 69; and evil, 121–22; and God's project, 120, 124, 125; help sinners, 146; humanity, 123, 153, 154; impersonal and personal, 8; individual, 135; Luther on, 165n34; and the noosphere, 60, 174n85; of omission, 79, 124–25; original, 151, 152, 153, 154–58, 176n1; passivities, 18–19; social, 130–34, 135–36, 174n83, 174n85; systemic, 133; traditional view, 7, 123, 124, 151
Sladek, Ursula, 99
Slavery, 133–34
Smith, Fred, 90–97
Smoke Rise Baptist Church, 77–78
Society, 133
Solar energy, 99
Spiritual exercises, 75–76, 78, 82, 83, 86, 91, 95–96, 101, 107–8, 112–13, 115, 118, 120, 123–24, 126, 129, 133, 136, 141, 145, 147
Spiritual Exercises (Loyola), 48
Spirituality: anxiety, 46; evolved, 21–22; group-focused, 54; Ignatius Loyola, 48; listening to the Spirit, 161n5; traditional, 21, 46, 54
Spiritualization, 35
Suffering, 27, 55–56, 70–71, 153, 169n11
Sure thing, 86

Teresa of Avila, 38
Thomism, 62
Time Has Come, The, 117

187